FREEDOM

D1412375

FREEDOM

TWELVE LIVES TRANSFORMED
BY THE THEOLOGY OF THE BODY

EDITED BY
MATTHEW PINTO

INTRODUCTION BY
CHRISTOPHER WEST

ASCENSION PRESS

West Chester, Pennsylvania

Ascension Press
Post Office Box 1990
West Chester, PA 19380
Orders: 1-800-376-0520
www.AscensionPress.com

Cover design: DesignWorks Group, Sisters, Oregon

Printed in the United States of America
12 11 10 9 8 7 6 5 4 3 2 1

ISBN 978-1-934217-45-0

To my friend Christopher West.

Praise God for the gifts He has given you and how you have used them for the Kingdom. Thank you for your integrity and humility. You are a great gift to the world, the Church, and to my apostolate, my marriage, and my family. I look forward to many years of laboring in the vineyard with you.

Contents

Introduction

Christopher West

One of my favorite things about traveling the world and sharing the glorious vision of life and love found in John Paul II's Theology of the Body (TOB) is the fine people I meet along the way. I much prefer to stay in family homes rather than in hotels and to have people meet me at the airport rather than rent a car. And I am always on the lookout for people who might want to join me for a bite to eat after a seminar. I marvel at the story that is each and every human life. What an *honor*, what a *privilege* to be welcomed into the heart of another, to share in that person's joys and hopes, triumphs and tragedies, hurts and healings.

As I often say in my lectures, I would love to be able to sit down with each and every person on the planet so that we might get to know each other and share our stories. Of course, time and space do not allow for that here on earth. But heaven will. In heaven, we won't be limited by time and space. God willing, I will *know* you and your life's story, and you will *know* me and mine. We will be enriched by each other in a unique way—because each of us has a unique story to share.

This heavenly reality of the perfect enrichment of each and everyone by each and everyone else has a name—the communion of saints. In a way beyond our wildest imaginings, and in a way that floods us with everlasting peace and rejoicing, one day we will see all and be seen by all; we will know all and be known by all; and God will be all in all (see Ephesians 1:23). Meanwhile, here on earth, we only get little glimpses into people's lives—and relatively few lives at that, considering all the human beings who have ever existed. But each glimpse into a person's life is a privilege. By seeing into the life of another, new perspectives open up, and new dimensions of our humanity can be awakened. That is one of the great blessings of this book. By seeing how God's grace has worked in the lives of others, our own lives are greatly enriched.

Theology of the Body Is for Every-body

The lives of the men and women you will meet in these pages have all been profoundly shaped by their encounter with John Paul II's Theology of the Body. (If you are unfamiliar with the Theology of the Body, see the appendix for a brief overview of its main themes.) Some are married, others are single, and still others are consecrated celibates. This brings up a critical point.

The Theology of the Body is often considered an extended teaching on marriage and sexual love. It is that, to be sure. But it is also *so much more*. Building on the mystical tradition of the Church, the Theology of the Body approaches the union of spouses as a "lens" through which to view the whole reality of God's plan for humanity. Studying the body as a *theology*, then, "concerns the whole Bible" (TOB 69:8) and plunges us into "the perspective of the whole gospel, of the whole teaching, even more, of the whole mission of Christ" (TOB 49:3).

Hence, what we learn in the Theology of the Body is obviously "important with regard to marriage," John Paul tells us. However, it "is equally essential and *valid for the [understanding] of man* in general: for the fundamental problem of understanding him and for the self-understanding of his being in the world" (TOB 102:5). This is why the Theology of the Body is not only for married couples. The theology *of the body* is for every-*body*. It is for everybody who is hungry for the meaning of life. As John Paul II observes, within the context of sexual love, the Theology of the Body affords "the rediscovery of the meaning of the whole of existence, of the meaning of life" (TOB 46:6).

How I Discovered the Theology of the Body

Perhaps the most frequent question I'm asked in my lectures is "How did you get involved in promoting the Theology of the Body?" Like most people, I can remember from a very early age being amazed by the difference between the sexes. When that God-given curiosity is not met in healthy, holy ways—that is, with a proper, ongoing formation in God's glorious, beautiful, wonderful plan for making us male and female—we inevitably seek to satisfy that curiosity in unhealthy, unholy ways. That is the story of my childhood and teen years in nutshell. Having been "evangelized" by the likes of Hugh Hefner, I followed what the world told me would satisfy my hunger. The wounds from several years of unchaste living, however, would catch up with me in college. The fervent prayers of my mother were eventually answered when, at the age of twenty, after a painful breakup with a long-time girlfriend, I experienced a profound encounter with Christ and returned to the practice of the Catholic faith.

At the time, my family was involved in a covenant community—an outgrowth of the charismatic renewal where families, single people, and priests and religious committed themselves to a common way of life, prayer, and worship. When it came to relationships between the sexes, though, this way of life left *much* to be desired. An entire generation of young people had been raised in this particular community with a notion of "holiness" that either negated or held in deep suspicion even the most normal manifestations of sexual attraction. I had experienced firsthand the harmful effects of society's indulgent approach to sex. But this approach—promoted in the name of following Christ—also seemed very unhealthy to me. Is sexual repression the only possible response to sexual license? I wanted answers. I wanted to know why God gave us sexual attraction in the first place. If I could, I wanted to get to the bottom of the whole male-female "thing."

So, at the age of twenty-one, I devoted myself to an intense study of all the key texts of Scripture that spoke of God's plan for making us male and female and calling us to become "one flesh." For more than two years, I dedicated a solid chunk of time each day to praying through Genesis 1-4; the Song of Songs; Matthew 5, 19, and 22; I Corinthians 7 and 11; and Ephesians 5, among others. In the course of my study, a grand "nuptial vision" began to emerge. The spousal analogy of the Scriptures came to life for me; I was coming to see my Catholic faith in an entirely new way. It shed light on the entire mystery of our creation, fall, and redemption in Christ.

It seemed the whole reason God created us as male and female was to reveal his own mysterious plan to "marry" us (see Hosea 2:19)— to become "one flesh" with us in Christ (see Ephesians 5:31-32). In turn, this "nuptial vision" helped me to understand all the seemingly obscure and controversial teachings of the Church. I fell in love with the Eucharist, the body of the New Adam. I fell in love with Mary, the New Eve. I came to see that the male-female "thing" is right at the heart of the whole beauty and splendor of the Catholic faith. This new understanding set me on *fire*. Moreover, it set me *free* from the lies that had formed me growing up.

When I began sharing this "nuptial vision" with some of the leaders of the covenant community, though, I was met with blank stares or worse. One person insinuated that the amount of time I was devoting to the issues of God's plan for man and woman could only be a source of distraction from my relationship with Christ. I was baffled. *Distraction from Christ? My study had only inflamed my love for Christ.* It seemed to me that the very purpose of sex and marriage was to lead us to Christ. I knew that I would forever need to grow in a deeper understanding of this "great mystery," but I was also convinced that I was onto something essential.

One night—September 26, 1993, to be exact, a night I remember well—a family friend came over to my parent's home for dinner. I knew she had studied some theology, so I thought I would test out a bit of my "nuptial vision" on her. To my surprise, the first words out of her mouth were, "You must have read John Paul II's Theology of the Body." "Theology of what ... ?," I responded. "What's that?" She said, "Gosh, it sounds like you already read it. You're talking like John Paul II." *You've got to be kidding me,* I thought. I pressed her to tell me more. She told me it was published by the Daughters of St. Paul, and she gave me a phone number to order it, which I did first thing the next day.

When it arrived in the mail, I devoured it in a matter of weeks. Not only did I find confirmation of what I had learned in my own study of the very same Scripture passages, but the Pope's reflections took me to an entirely new level of understanding this great "spousal mystery." I remember thinking that somehow I had chanced upon the long-lost treasure that every person yearns for, the path to the banquet of love that truly satisfies the hungers of the human heart. Perhaps it was youthful idealism (I was just twenty-three at the time) or delusions of grandeur, but I truly believed that somehow, for some reason, I was privy to a kind of divine secret that had the potential to transform the whole world, and I needed to do something about it. I sensed then that I would spend the rest of my life studying this mystical "theology of the body," entering more deeply into it, and sharing its riches with the world. Thus began my mission and career as a "theologian of the body."

It has been quite a journey. The most difficult part has been taking all this grand theology from my head to my heart. Knowing it is one thing; living it is another. Thankfully, God is patient and forgiving. And thank God I have a patient, forgiving wife.

A New Sexual Revolution

All these years later, it is exciting to see how a new movement is gaining momentum in the Catholic Church and beyond. I'm grateful to God that, despite numerous missteps and mistakes along the way, He has allowed me to play a part in that. Several of the individuals whose stories are chronicled in this book mention my work as their first exposure with the Theology of the Body. Nonetheless, I would like to make it clear that the credit goes to a great many people —scholars, catechists, and "ordinary" Catholics in the pew—who have dedicated themselves to helping the Church at various levels "break open" the great treasure John Paul has bequeathed us. Many were on the scene teaching Theology of the Body long before I was —people like Monsignor Lorenzo Albacete, Father Richard Hogan, Mary Beth Bonacci, and Janet Smith (among others)—and I owe a great deal of my inspiration to them.

If we read the "signs of the times," we will realize that the "Theology of the Body phenomenon" is not a fad. God is doing something powerful in people's lives. A new sexual revolution is underway. It can be likened to the revolution that brought down the Iron Curtain—spreading slowly and quietly in human hearts that welcomed the truth that this Polish pope proclaimed about the human person. When that revolution of the heart hit critical mass, the Berlin Wall fell quickly, suddenly. The dehumanizing totalitarian ideology of communism that supported it for thirty years simply couldn't stand in the face of a great multitude of people who had glimpsed their true dignity. I believe it will be similar with the Theology of the Body revolution. The predominant pornographic ideology will collapse —perhaps quickly, even suddenly—when enough men and women realize who they really are and to what bodily glory the en-fleshed God calls us.

God willing, the revolution may even reach Hugh Hefner. If we could find a way to put it in a language he could understand, that he just might say, "That's what I've been looking for all along." After all, isn't he, like everyone else, just searching to satisfy the "ache" within his heart? In the end, the difference between great sinners and great saints is where they go to satisfy their ache. In the twelve stories you are about to read, you will find ordinary men and women like you who have found something extraordinary in John Paul II's Theology of the Body—something that corresponds to their deep, personal "ache." A great hope has been awakened in each of them, and a great *freedom*. I encourage you to allow their stories to awaken hope in you.

Perhaps you have wondered if there really is a love that corresponds to the longings of your heart. Perhaps you have wondered if all the pain and hurt that life dishes out is normal, and if learning to cope with sin and dysfunction is all you can hope for. Perhaps you have done what you considered the "good religious thing" and found your spirit confined or oppressed. Or perhaps you rebelled against religion altogether and found the ways of the world wanting. Some of you may be struggling to know what vocation God has for you, while others might be struggling with the vocation you have already chosen. Wherever you are in your journey, there is much comfort and inspiration to be found in the lives of the twelve who in this book have generously shared their journey with us. May they help you find *freedom*.

Christopher West is recognized around the world for his work promoting an integral, biblical vision of human life, love, and sexuality. Christopher is the best-selling author of five books and one of the most sought-after speakers in the Church today, having delivered more than 1,000 public lectures on four continents, in ten countries, and in nearly 200 American cities. He serves as a research fellow and faculty member of the Theology of the Body Institute near Philadelphia. He has also lectured on a number of other prestigious faculties, offering graduate and undergraduate courses at St. John Vianney Seminary in Denver, the John Paul II Institute in Melbourne, Australia, and the Institute for Priestly Formation at Creighton University in Omaha. Christopher and his wife, Wendy, live with their five children near Lancaster, Pennsylvania.

Longing for the One

Rose Sweet

Patrick leaned over and whispered in my ear, "Come with me." I caught a warm whiff of his cologne, and my heart skipped a beat. We were having dinner with friends, and the others were chatting noisily when Patrick pushed his chair back, stood up, and silently offered me his hand. I took it. The others didn't seem to notice us as he led me away from the table.

I had met Patrick just a few weeks before, at a singles' dance at our parish, and before the night was over he asked if he could call me. I recall his piercing dark eyes framed with black hair and the faint smell of his leather jacket practically inviting me into his arms. *Stop it*, I thought, *Get a hold of yourself!* I had been deeply hurt by divorce—more than once—and been single for more than ten years. I wasn't anxious to be in a relationship just for the sake of dating. I thought I had it all under control, but with those flutters and goosebumps, my body was definitely responding in a way I had not felt in many years.

As soon as we had left the dining room and rounded the corner, Patrick stopped, pulled me into his arms, and kissed me long and hard on the lips. "I've been waiting all night to do that," Patrick whispered as he held me. He smiled and kissed me again. I couldn't speak. After I excused myself to go and check my lipstick, I practically floated back to the dining room. When I returned to the table, his brother, Mike, looked at me and said, "Wow, Rose, you have quite a blush . . . where *were* you guys?"

I just smiled and my face flushed. I was unable to eat another bite. There is something about "love" that fills you up to the brim, quenching your thirst and satisfying your appetite. Patrick seemed perfect. The long dormant hope in my heart began to sprout strong, green shoots. This relationship, though, would take an interesting twist, but more on that later.

Hey, This is My Body

For a long time I hadn't much hope of being in love and married because of my painful past. I had grown up in the turmoil of the sixties where millions of my generation were hell-bent on breaking free of the Catholic Church's chains we felt had bound us for too long. I was an enlightened child of the sexual revolution. Who were *they* to tell me what I could do with *my* body?

But despite the culture's strong pull away from traditional relationships, I had always longed deeply for a husband, home, and children. Being thin and beautiful would get a man to notice me, fall hopelessly in love with me, and then marry me. Or so I thought.

I found myself acting like a wife with every boyfriend, waiting painfully for the proposals that never came. Was something wrong with me because I could not disconnect my heart the way some women could, casually coming and going in and out of relationships with apparent ease? Maybe I just had not met the right man yet. And because I eventually came to see that it was really Christ my heart desired, in a certain sense that was true.

Looking for Any Body

The years flew by, and I found myself pushing harder for the husband, home, and children I felt were my right but which kept eluding me. By the time I was in my mid-thirties, I had two failed marriages: the first, to a man named John, had been an escape plan to move out of what I felt was a miserable childhood home. I had manipulated myself into a nine-month "marriage" to an abusive alcoholic husband. My divorce was granted due to the newly established "irreconcilable differences." I moved back home temporarily, and my parents urged me to seek an annulment from the Church. Whatever. In my immaturity and ignorance, it meant little to me.

Ashamed of my failure and scared of being hurt again, I didn't start dating again for a few years. Actually, dating probably isn't the right word. Having unmarried sex is more like it. Like most of my girlfriends, I rationalized that I was not a "loose" woman if I was only in a relationship with one man at a time. Despite my wounded heart, the desire for love drove me right into the arms of Jim, a handsome naval officer, and I quickly became pregnant. Unwed motherhood was still a social stigma, but I was secretly thrilled. I had wanted to get married and have children, and now I could have both. I knew he would "do the right thing" and marry me right away. He didn't.

His commanding officer advised him to reject marriage as a threat to his career plans and deny paternity as well. I was stunned and deeply hurt. Pregnant and abandoned, I was asked by my parish to stop teaching catechism classes and forced to resign as an extraordinary minister of the Eucharist. More shame. Although some were surprised that I still went to church after such treatment, I had always kept my childlike love for Jesus and His Mother, Mary. The graces from my baptism and confirmation were undoubtedly still present, small glowing embers amidst the ashes of my sins and the stench of the culture in which I had chosen to live. I had been abandoned alright . . . but not by God.

I eventually ignored my heartache and focused on the joy of my baby boy, who I had felt kicking and whom I had seen on the ultrasound. I named him Charlie and, while pregnant, bought his first little blue blanket and a baby book. But after six months, I woke up during the night in labor and in the morning I lost my baby. Numb and in shock, I tried to ignore my shame and sorrow, still determined to get that husband, home, and children I thought I deserved. So I bought my first house and adopted a little school-aged girl whom the state agency couldn't seem to place. That was it. I was more than halfway there. Now all I needed was a man.

Poor Dave. I manipulated him right to the altar. Just eighteen, my second husband was much younger than I and had been abandoned by his father at a tender age. He was eager to be part of a family again. I thrust him into the role of husband and father when he was barely past puberty himself. My heart was no longer reaching out for a husband, home, and children . . . it was greedily grasping. We struggled for a few years, our delicate and disordered relationship torn apart by nasty psychological issues and a problem child. The adoption agency had failed to advise us of the extent of our daughter's deeply troubled past. We struggled for almost three years with her problems that affected us and the rest of our family. At the recommendation of a leading psychiatrist, she was placed in a group home where she received intense counseling and lived until she was eighteen.

I felt I was a failure at being a mother, and when Dave moved out shortly after, I faced another failed marriage as well. Dave sought an annulment, and I was starting to see that maybe I had some problems I needed to face. I finally got some counseling and began reading self-help books in an effort to identify the source of my pain, but I was still living an "unsurrendered" life. Not long after Dave, I met Tom.

Tom had just divorced his wife and had a two-year old son, Mikey, who leapt into my arms the day we met. They fit perfectly into the picture frame of my dream. We married outside the Church because I couldn't wait for what I thought were empty formalities. Our first year was nothing more than legal lust, the beginning of a ten-year struggle to make a marriage out of emotional problems, bitter struggles in court with his ex-wife, counseling that didn't seem to work, and all our savings spent on infertility treatments. We attended Mass faithfully, and Mikey even became an altar boy, but we were like children: obedient in some areas and rebellious in others. I knew the Church had some objection to in-vitro fertilization, but I had no idea what it was and frankly I didn't care. I had no interest in learning more about my faith. I wanted a baby. The Bible says babies are a blessing. What could be wrong with that?

Sacrificing My Body

After painful injections, costly drugs, and numerous trips to a fertility clinic, I produced fourteen eggs in one menstrual cycle. They were extracted by a long needle and fertilized in a Petri dish in the back room of the clinic with sperm my husband had "donated" by masturbating to pornography in the doctor's restroom. The next day the nurse called and reported that eleven of the eggs had fertilized and she asked if I wanted to come see them. In a quiet, dark room I stepped up to the microscope and stared down at the eleven human persons. I was excited and scared at the same time, thinking, *What on earth have you done, Rose?* Doctors had confirmed that my womb was defective so my sister had agreed to be a surrogate. But a few weeks after the procedure, her period started, which told us that the tiny embryos had been unable to implant and continue growing. At this news I dropped to the doctor's office floor and wailed uncontrollably. I was in my early forties, and now I was out of money and out of time. My newly-formed babies were dead—and so were my chances of ever having my own children.

Something inside me finally shattered. The scales began to fall from my eyes and I saw my life's painful patterns. My sins were staring me in the face and for the first time I was staring right back at them. I knew I needed to fall before God and beg His forgiveness. A deep yearning for Him welled inside my chest. Little did I know how sacramental this next move was—the body making my invisible penitence visible—but I flung myself face first, arms outstretched, and dramatically prostrate on my bed. The words came silently on their own, *O my God, I am heartily sorry for having offended Thee* ... and I offered Him every area of my life.

In that act of surrender I expected to feel differently, to hear bells, or to maybe sense the presence of angels. There was nothing like that. So I slowly got up, turned on the TV, and made myself a bowl of yogurt. Little did I know that in that precious and intimate act of communion with God, I had conceived new spiritual life and that little dying ember in my heart was beginning to fan into a blazing flame.

Saint Paul tells us in his letter to the Romans to offer our bodies as a living sacrifice (see Romans 12:1-2), but I must have skipped the part where he tells us to brace ourselves for things getting worse. Although I was beginning to live a life where Christ was the center, my marriage—which had been flawed from the beginning—did not survive. When my husband decided to leave, I again lost everything. What I did not lose was my ever-growing faith in God and the knowledge He was with me through it all, promising to bring something beautiful out of the ashes.

A More Beautiful Body

After a third divorce and the loss of a baby boy, an adopted daughter, a stepson, and children through in vitro, I quit pursuing my dreams and sought to pursue Christ even more. My non-Catholic friends had always encouraged me in my personal relationship with Jesus, but it was the Catholic Church who called me into full communion with His Body and the gifts of the sacraments. In surrendering my heart to Christ I willingly surrendered to His Church as well. With a good confession and completing the annulment process for all of my attempted marriages, I came home to stay. I was still in my forties and hopeful that God could still do great things in me. Immediately, I began to have an insatiable hunger for a deeper knowledge of Scripture, of the Church's teachings, and of the lives of the saints. St. John of the Cross and St. Teresa of Avila opened up for me the concept of a mystical marriage with Christ and I loved it! Wasn't romance, love, and marriage been what I had pursued all along?

A few years went by, and, as I neared fifty years old, all the longings for love I'd always had were still there as strong as ever. One night in prayer, as I was reflecting on my past life, I asked God to show me why all my life I had been nearly crazy with a desire for love, sex, and marriage. *Please show me,* I asked, *why this is so all-consuming and powerful, not just for me but for so many people I know.* I thought of the mystical marriage and I knew: everything we long for, everything we desire is really a desire for Christ. Everything in creation is somehow meant to point us to heaven. If that was true, then could it be that what made us read romance novels, watch weepy chick-flicks, and put on our "cha-cha" heels be a desire for Jesus? I could hardly stand it. I didn't *want* human sex to be about God! Somehow I thought the two could never mix. I eventually drifted off to a restless sleep. But a few days later I would read the book *Theology of the Body,* a collection of Pope John Paul II's Wednesday audiences, for the first time . . . and my life would never be the same.[1]

A Sweet and Simple Logic

The teachings of the Theology of the Body are deep and profound, but it is also sweet and simple. It asks and answers the same three questions my Dad often used to tell us kids we needed to ask ourselves. I can see him now, in his leather chair, puffing on his two-dollar cigar, saying to me, "Rosie, you're growing up. There's a time you'll need to stop and seriously ask your self: *Where did I come from, where am I going, and how do I get there?*"

Then my father would tell me I was put on this earth to love God and to do His will, but that did not sound very fun to me. Thinking about Eden seemed too abstract. It was so long ago. And heaven was too far away. I was here, and I wanted to be happy now. A handsome husband, a beautiful home, and lots of kids were heaven to me . . . and

---

[1] The revised version of these addresses is now available under the title *Man and Woman He Created Them: A Theology of the Body* (Boston: Pauline, 2006), edited by Dr. Michael Waldstein.

that is what I blindly pursued. So in a way Dad was wrong: I wasn't very grown up at all.

The Theology of the Body revealed Scripture to me in a way that made sense of my own life's experiences and helped me mature mentally, emotionally, and spiritually. John tells us at the end of his gospel that the world could not contain the books of Jesus' unrecorded words and deeds. I think the blessings that will keep coming to me— and the whole world—from John Paul II's Theology of the Body will be as countless.

Who Are We?

I discovered in the reading of this extraordinary work that we are persons made to come into a loving and perfect communion with God and others. For most of my adult life, I had left God out. I had been duped into thinking human love was all I needed for happiness. Love for and from others is meant to help us experience a taste of God's love, but it is no replacement! There is only one Love that completely satisfies. But once we realize that, how do we find it? How do we live it?

A loving parent would never leave his children lost in a dark world without some way to get home. Hansel and Gretel only had crumbs, but we wandering, wounded sons and daughters have millions of signs that point us to our heavenly home. I came to realize that the glory of creation, the beauty of nature, the sound of music—and even love and sex—are some ways that people begin to see that there is something spectacular and mysterious to which we are called. But sadly, I (and likely most of us) never look past these "crumbs" and stay stuck worshiping the signs.

The Theology of the Body made me realize that my own female

body was God's first sign to show me the way home. John Paul II said that man finds himself in the sincere gift of himself. Since my first boyfriend in high school, I had given my heart away to others, and my body to even more. It hadn't brought me long lasting happiness but it did bring deep emotional wounds and shame. Like most, I really didn't know what sincere and authentic love was. Who could show me? I realized with new ideas that it was Christ. I knew Jesus was the savior, the founder of the Church, my friend, my teacher. But now I could also see Him as my chaste lover who had already given me His body out of the most perfect love—first on other cross and continually every day in the Eucharist. Other men had given me their body, but not their hearts. With my intellect, emotions, and imagination—and from the remembered tender touches I'd had through my body—I could move more closely into an intimate experience of Christ in my thoughts, my prayers, even the way I thought about myself as a woman who was always deeply loved.

The Theology of the Body keeps pointing us to Christ. I cannot count the number of my non-Catholic friends who try to remind me that Christ is risen, insisting almost with disgust that we Catholics need to get him off that cross. But at that very moment—bloodied and nailed on the cross—He showed the deepest love for me and for many. I know now that *that* was the hour of True Love. Seeing His crucified image reminds of me the intensity of that love. We women dream of a man who so adores us that he would not hesitate to take a bullet for us. Most of us would agree that flowers, candy, and romantic trips pale in comparison to the willingness to suffer and sacrifice for one we love. Every person longs for that kind of love whether they admit it or not. It was Christ who took that bullet—and a crown of thorns as well. The Theology of the Body helped me to see that, despite the way book or movie heroes might appear to love women, I have always wanted a man who could love me as Christ loves. And now that I am finally growing up, I long to love to that same depth.

The Spousal Analogy

Saints and mystics throughout the years have written of their "spousal union" with God. Similarly, John Paul II reminds us that God repeatedly revealed Himself to His people as their Husband, and that Christ came as Bridegroom to the Church. Marriage between a man and a woman is meant to image that loving union between God and mankind.

Our bodies are *not* things, and sexual union is *not* a recreational act. Only when I read the Theology of the Body did it finally sink in: It is God who truly satisfies, and sex points the way. God has always desired to woo us and wed us. So my fierce longing to be in love, to have sex, and to be married was in some way a perfectly good desire, albeit one twisted by my own selfishness. And following this beautiful imagery, my longing for children also has a deeper dimension of the desire to be filled and made "pregnant" with divine life and love that I could bring into the world.

My call as a woman to be "wed" to God, to be one-flesh with Him, and to bear His life and love to the world is stamped right in my body. My breasts are a sign *and* a reality that I am to nurture and "feed" others with the most tender of care, and—as mothers know—that means even sacrificially, even when you feel like you have not one drop left. My womb is a holy place, not just a fleshly incubator. It is a holy-of-holies, the secret place where heaven and earth unite and new life is formed. It is also an image of the human heart: meant to be open, to be filled with life and love, and to carry that divine life into the world . . . even when morning sickness, pain, and blood come with it. My body testifies to all of mankind as to the bridal posture we should assume before a loving God.

Spousal Love is Free, Total, Faithful, and Fruitful

John Paul II gives us a practical way of living out this kind of spousal love. "Go to Jesus," he seems to say over and over, because He is the model for a love that is free, total, faithful, and fruitful. But would my love transition from the grasping and selfishness that had characterized me for so long? After living with this teaching for a while, I began to consistently use these four points to test my attitude and actions.

Christ's love is given *freely*. He has no hidden agenda, no selfish motives. He gives knowing exactly what He is doing. There is no force or pressure in His total gift of self to the world, His Bride. He gave His life of his own accord. I began to see that most men in my life were never "free" to love me rightly. They were like me—in bondage to lust, fears, loneliness, or neediness.

Christ loves *totally*, with nothing held back. His love is radical and irrevocable. Given without measure and permanently available. Loving totally implies permanence and totality in all areas of life. When a man wants to sleep with me but will not make me his wife or share his home with me or protect me legally and financially, then he is only giving part of himself and rejecting part of me. This is not loving totally. So why would I settle for that any longer?

Christ loves *faithfully*, never, ever inviting any harm to come to

His Beloved. To some degree, sex outside marriage always deprives the parties of respect, security, trust, fullness, and the freedom that comes with a real love. Even sex inside marriage can be "unfaithful" if it is selfish or lustful.

Christ loves *fruitfully*, never closing the body or the heart to the gift of life. Children can be a huge challenge, and many people deliberately close their bodies off to the possibility of new life during sex. That lack of openness is also a rejection of the whole person: I want you, but not the gift of your fertility. Like sexual bulimia, they want the good taste but spit out the fruit. And the opposite occurs, too: I began to understand that children (new human persons!) are indeed the fruit of a loving union between spouses, not to be artificially forced in a lab dish so that an adult's emotional hunger can be filled.

I came to see that the only human relationship that is full, total, faithful, and fruitful is marriage between one man and one woman, two who are called to become one and who bring the highest level of complementarity possible. Anything less can have elements of love and truth, but it is not marriage, and sometimes it is not love at all. And sex? I came to see sex as a visible sign of the covenant of spousal love, rather than as the act that follows dinner and a movie on the third date. Too many of us say "I do" with our genitals, but we say "I don't" with our heart. No wonder we have so much spiritual schizophrenia!

This is My Body, Given for You

I once read a funny tombstone at the *Ripley's Believe it or Not* museum in San Francisco:

HERE LIES SOLOMON PEAS

Peas ain't here, only the pod.

Peas shelled out, went home to God.

Too many people have mistakenly thought that the body is just a shell we discard after death. It is through our bodies, though, and in particular married sexual union, that we can authentically image God's free, total, faithful, and fruitful love.

During creation, God said that our bodies are very good. For years, I often hated the image I saw in the mirror, but now (most of the time!) I can look past the imperfections and celebrate that with my body I can hold someone's hand, pat them on the back, kiss them, tickle them, or look into their eyes. I can work hard, laugh loudly, and respond to the world around me. The Theology of the Body helped me see that it is through my body that I can show Him love in return and even be made holier in sharing in His sufferings. My body may not look "very good" by cultural standards, but the things I can do with my body can be very, very good!

The Liturgy Has a Nuptial Dimension

The Theology of the Body taught me in profound ways about the nuptial mystery of Jesus as the Bridegroom. I came to see, though, that this spousal analogy eventually falls short of the real thing but it helps us see that marriage is actually a participation in this great mystery. In marriage we have the capacity to not only image but truly enter into and participate in the one, perfect love of a Jesus for His Bride. Again . . . wow!

When I was young, the nuns taught us that the Mass was the unbloody sacrifice of Calvary, where, having died once for all, Christ allows us to transcend space and time, as it were, and mysteriously enter into that same, single sacrifice and offer ourselves with Him to the Father. But I thought, *Who wants to climb up on a cross and die if Jesus already did?* My non-Catholic friends kept saying we didn't have to go to the cross because He already did. But I began to see that going to the cross—as Christ commands—is the only way to show the deepest love. The Theology of the Body helped me see that it was the romantic element of the liturgy that had eluded me for so long. The meal is a *wedding banquet*. The sacrifice is that of a *Lover for His Beloved*. It is a supreme, heroic, unselfish, passionate act of love by the God-man for the beautiful Bride—us—he cherished and wanted to rescue. Talk about romance! And that act of perfect love is eternally open to every generation who seeks it.

If Jesus is the Bridegroom who comes to rescue, woo, and wed His Bride, then everything about Him has a nuptial dimension, including the liturgy. This made me want to learn more about the Mass and to participate more meaningfully. I used to dread the "long part" before Communion, but now I see it in a new light—like quiet time before bed, or a long, meaningful talk with a spouse—and now it sometimes rushes by.

Once I realized how intimate and sweet this exchange is meant to be, I began to desire it more than once a year at Christmas or Easter, and even more than once a week on Sundays. That's why I find myself more frequently up early and off to morning Mass where I'm not going to some thing, I am going to some *body!*

In the church pew I often reflect that today I will join my life with Christ's in His perfect sacrifice, which is also my act of love for Him, but I will also meet the Lover of my soul. It's for good reason that I still long to walk up the aisle and be given away. I understand now that all my longings for a husband are at their very core not just a longing for God (as some ethereal being) but a *real person* who had a real body, the God-Man, Jesus. I am going to enter the most intimate communion with Him in the Eucharist.

During Mass, my mind will sometimes flood with images of warm embraces and a "one flesh" union and the desire I had always had for such love. Some days when I feel distant from Him or am just "not in the mood" I know that it's okay because all marriages have those times. The Mass has many dimensions, the Passover Meal, the Sacrifice on Calvary, but also the Divine Romance. After all, it is the Bridegroom who dies for His Bride and calls us to the Wedding Feast and then to live out a long life together. Do we think there is no passion, nor romance to that most sublime love story?

A Love that Satisfies

Remember Patrick, who led me away from the table to give me a kiss? I found out a few dates later that we had very different views on important things. After a few discussions where I invited him to explore our faith together, he made it quite clear he really had no interest in the path I had taken to deeper intimacy with God. I knew what I had to do. Goodbyes are painful. Part of me didn't want to, but I know to have continued would only have used him to fill my loneliness . . . and I never again want to do that to another human being.

After I ended our relationship, I wallowed in dark chocolate and depression, but I was joyful at the same time because I knew that I was finally living out the principles of the Theology of the Body. It is as if not Patrick but Christ has whispered my ear, "Come with me" and that I have been given the grace to get up and go with Him.

It is Christ who wants to draw me into His arms.
It is Christ who knows how to love me.
It is Christ who wants to fill my life with children.

Do I still long for a man to love? Sure I do. But my desire no longer controls me and the greater desire to love rightly has taken root.

What about children? I have many. For the last decade I have been blessed with a growing apostolate for singles and the divorced all over the world who read my books or see or hear me on DVDs and CDs. I counsel and encourage those who are facing annulments. I travel around the country where I can meet and "mother" many, with a smile, a hug, or even a word of wisdom. It warms my heart to know that from my own failures and losses, I can always offer a mother's love and encouragement through the tough times in their lives.

I consider myself a bit like Dorothy in the *Wizard of Oz*. She discovered that, in wearing the ruby red slippers, she always had the power to get what she wanted. I, too, had run away from "home" in search of a husband, home, and children. The Theology of the Body has helped me see what I never really knew: *That I had what my heart desired all along.*

Rose Sweet is a Catholic author, teacher, and motivational speaker who seeks to offer real solutions for people with real problems, based on the spiritual treasures found in the Church - especially the Theology of the Body. A "divorce recovery coach" and the director of Sacred Heart Catholic Singles Incorporated, Rose is the author of the books How to Be First in a Second Marriage, A Woman's Guide: Healing the Heartbreak of Divorce, Healing the Divorced Heart, *and* Dear God, Send Me a Soul Mate. *Rose lives in the Palm Springs, California area. For more information, visit www.rosesweet.com.*

Living Only Half the Story

Katrina J. Zeno

The world would be a hilarious, even dangerous, place if we didn't understand what things are designed for. I might try to use toilet paper to design a dress or gasoline to boil potatoes or marshmallows to build a bridge. If so, you would do the public a great service to call the authorities and have me locked away. But don't reach for your cell phone yet.

For years, I never thought about the meaning and purpose of the body. In other words, what is the body designed for? Of course, I understood that I could use my body to accomplish difficult tasks—like biking forty-plus miles for a charity bike-a-thon when I was thirteen or graduating as valedictorian of my high school class. Both of these required tremendous amounts of physical effort and self-discipline.

But that's where my understanding stopped. It never crossed my mind that my body could have a spiritual or even theological meaning. That was the domain of the soul. After all, Jesus came to save souls, not bodies (or so I thought). When I sinned, it was my soul that was affected—tainted, so to speak. In heaven, my soul would see God face-to-face. In the meantime, my body was simply a convenient shell to house my soul until my spirit was finally liberated at death. Hallelujah! I would shed my body like a snakeskin and finally be free!

Without realizing it, I was a closet Platonist. Plato taught that the soul was the true nature of the person and the body was incidental to one's personhood. In fact, the body served like a prison for the soul. Therefore, our human perfection was the liberation of the soul from the prison of the body so that it could exist in a purely spiritual state. Yup, I was a true-blue Platonist. But suffering changed all that.

I like to think that I had a near perfect childhood (if there is such a thing). I was born and raised in beautiful San Diego in a wonderful, Catholic home. I happily swam, body surfed, and danced my way through grade school and high school. A year after graduation, I married my high school sweetheart; ten years later, my life was in a shambles from a failed marriage.

How could this have happened? I prayed; I loved God; I had graduated with top theology honors from Franciscan University of Steubenville. Weren't these the guarantees of a successful marriage? My Platonism was peeking through. I had assumed that the spiritual dimension could trump everything else. Despite the emotional wounds that our bodies harbored, I thought these could be minimized or at least relegated to the periphery with enough prayer and good intentions. I had unconsciously contributed to a greater division between body and spirit rather than a deeper integration and harmony between the two, with painful results.

Suddenly, I was everything I had never wanted to be: a single, working mom living with my son in Steubenville, Ohio. This was a bitter pill to swallow for someone who cherished sacramental marriage, large families, at-home mothering, and San Diego sunshine. Everything my identity hinged on evaporated in an instant. Who was I? Where was my life going? What is my value and worth if not drawn from life as a devoted Catholic wife welcoming and raising a quiver-full of children, as Psalm 127 states?

Enter Pope John Paul II, but not his Theology of the Body. This was 1990—ten years before the Theology of the Body became well-known in the United States. Instead, I came to the Theology of the Body through the back door—through Pope John Paul II's writings on women.

The Feminine Genius

Perhaps somewhere in my reams of spiritual journals is a note about how I first became aware of *Mulieris Dignitatem* ("On the Dignity and Vocation of Women"), but it's not accessible to my failing memory retrieval system (a common occupational hazard for women over forty). In any case, I devoured John Paul II's profound apostolic letter to women not once or twice but multiple times. I encountered for the first time the language of the "nuptial meaning" of the body (now referred to as the "spousal meaning" of the body), spiritual motherhood, and making a gift of self. My body ceased to be a functional, disposable tool and instead became an integral part of my feminine identity.

In particular, I realized that I had a distinctive gift of self to make *as a woman*, and this was indicated by my physiological structure: only women have an empty space within. Women are created to be receptive, to be life-givers. Women make a gift of self so that others can receive the gift of self—the gift of their very lives. And we don't do this in some abstract way, but precisely through the gift of our feminine bodies.

In God's carefully-thought-out design, the physical feminine body is a sign of a spiritual reality—that *all* women are called to motherhood. Indeed, while many are blessed with biological motherhood, all women are called to spiritual motherhood, to nurturing the emotional, moral, cultural, and spiritual lives of others. This distinctive feminine ability to make a gift of self is what John Paul II calls the "genius of woman."

Up to that point, I had never thought of women as having a feminine genius. On the contrary, I had unconsciously bought the lie that men and women were basically the same except for a couple of variant biological tweaks. Now John Paul II was making the bold claim that the bodies of men and women are distinctively different because they are linked to the way we make a distinctive masculine and feminine gift of self. Suddenly my body wasn't simply waiting in the wings as an optional understudy; it was taking center stage as the principal actor!

As I steeped myself in the language and concepts of *Mulieris Dignitatem*, the door to the Theology of the Body opened wide. I was already living the spousal meaning of the body through spiritual motherhood when I dove into the 129 addresses John Paul II delivered from 1979 to 1984. Of course, the language was difficult; of course, some of it didn't seem to make sense (some of the philosophical terms still leave me banging my head against the wall), but I guzzled John Paul II's incredible view of the human person and Trinitarian communion. In short, John Paul II changed my view of the Trinity from an old man in the sky, a young man, and a dove to a communion of self-giving love.

As You See God, So You See the World

My new perspective changed everything. And I do mean *everything*. Why? Because our image of God determines who we understand ourselves to be. Right from the beginning, Scripture reveals that we are made in God's image: "God created man in his image; in the divine image he created him; male and female he created them" (Genesis 1:27). Therefore, our concept of God directly influences our self concept.

For instance, if God is an old man in the sky who is not really interested or involved in our day-to-day lives, then what does this say about me? It says I am created to live aloof and detached from others and the world around me and basically bumble my way through life. But, if *God* is a communion of self-giving love, then that means *I* am created to live in a communion of self-giving love—whether I am single, married, divorced, two, forty-two, or 102!

I could wax eloquent on this wonderful mystery of the Trinity (or at least try to), but I want to go back to where I started: to the body. John Paul II's catecheses are subtitled "a theology of the body." Why? Why not "a theology of the soul"? If I had been giving them—which, thankfully, I was not—I would have focused on how our soul is made in God's image and likeness, on God as spirit, and, therefore, on how the spiritual part of us most closely resembles God. Sounds great, right?

Only half right. As human persons, we are told right from the beginning of Scripture that we image God by being both body and spirit (see Genesis 2, in which Adam is made from the clay of the ground and God's breath; "breath," in Hebrew, also means "spirit"). It is not only my spirit that images God, but my body as well. Big gulp! What a radically new thought for me. My body, my *feminine* body, images God? Yes, precisely because it is made for a gift of self. The Trinity is self-*giving* love: Father and Son pouring themselves out in gift to each other and that gift of love between them is a third Person; it *is* the Holy Spirit. My feminine body images God precisely when I pour myself out as a gift to others. The only way I can make a gift of self to others is through my body, not apart from it—precisely because all human actions, even those that have a spiritual dimension, are done through the body.

This catapulted me into a radically changed understanding of the body, *my* body. The only way I can image God is through my body, not apart from it. Jesus didn't come to save souls. He came to save *persons*, and that means my salvation will not be complete until soul *and* body are perfectly reunited in heaven and united to the Trinity. Another big gulp! You mean I don't get rid of my body? On the contrary, my feminine body will go with me all the way into eternity.

Thank goodness God didn't dump all these insights on me at once. Instead, they arrived in manageable chunks over a four- or five-year period. The final (and ongoing) result is that they have absolutely changed my understanding of the body, my body. My body is not a punishment or a prison, but a gift—and it is the way I make a gift of self to God and others. When others see my body, they not only should see me, but they also should see God.

If an alien landed in your backyard tonight and said to you, "I hear there's a God. What is God like?" And you said, "That's easy. Follow me around tomorrow, and you'll see." What would the alien conclude about God at the end of the day by observing you? I pray that he would conclude that God is patient and kind; He is not jealous; He does not put on airs, He is not self-seeking (see 1 Corinthians 13). This is the tremendous meaning and purpose of the body—to reveal God to the world every second of the day.

I have recently come to revel in the following idea: Many people are atheists because they say God can't exist due to the pain and suffering in the world. Wouldn't it be incredible if Christians lived the spousal meaning of the body (i.e., made a gift of self to everyone around them) in such a way that others concluded that God must exist because of the goodness, charity, and self-sacrificial love they observe? When the body becomes a theology, it becomes a clear sign and testimony that "God's love has been poured into our hearts through the Holy Spirit" (Romans 5:5) through our sincere self-giving.

Sacramental Sight

Without a doubt, the Theology of the Body has had a dramatic impact on my life. It changed my worldview from one where the material world is simply tolerated to one where the material world reveals God. Maybe that doesn't sound earth shattering to you, but for me it was a Copernican revolution. The center of my universe had been a purely *spiritual* existence; an on-going attempt to experience God apart from the physical world. Theology of the Body dismantled that approach and replaced it with a *sacramental* existence—seeing God revealed *through* the visible world rather than apart from it. Instead of distancing myself from the material world in order to be holy (a monastery in the Rocky Mountains with perpetual adoration would have been ideal), the whole world became a cathedral—a place to encounter God.

One of the most intriguing places where this shift occurred was in my experience of Argentine tango. For more than ten years I have danced Argentine tango as an artistic and cultural outlet. Being a devout Catholic, this hasn't always been easy since Argentine tango can be danced close, *very* close. (This can scandalize some, especially when it is viewed without the lens of the Theology of the Body.) Tango is often portrayed with great passion and intimacy. However, there is another side to tango, the hidden, sacramental side.

Danced in all its beauty and artistry, Argentine tango expresses the spousal meaning of the body in a visible way. As a couple dances, the man gives himself away to the woman, and the woman gives herself away to the man, and suddenly the two are no longer dancing as two, but as one. Right before our eyes we see union and communion, two and one, giving and receiving. The man and woman become a visible sign of the self-giving union between Christ and each of us.

I have come to call this type of approach to the world "sacramental sight"—striving to see the invisible through the visible. Nowhere have I been more challenged in this area than in the unclothed or scantily clad human body. This image was always an occasion for scandal for me, with a comfort factor of about negative 185. Why? Because I could see only naked body parts. I could not see beyond the physical dimension. However, as the Theology of the Body converted my mind and my sight, I began to see the body, even the naked human body, as the expression of the person who is made for a gift of self. I began to see a woman's breasts (I hope I don't offend anyone here) as a symbol of nourishment, life, and abundance.

Now, please do not misunderstand me. I am not advocating immodest dress or societal nakedness. What I am saying is that when I see a woman dressed immodestly, instead of letting it take me away from God, I use it as an occasion to redirect my thoughts to God: I thank Him for the breast as a divine symbol of life and nourishment, even while trying to help others understand the sacredness of the body and the need for appropriate attire.

Recently, I went to a massage appointment, and the "ample" receptionist had on a low-cut tank top. In the past, I would have interiorly fumed and been indignant at her inappropriate dress ("Doesn't she realize...?"). This time, when my massage was over, I asked for a manager and simply said, "I think a woman's breasts are very beautiful, but they are not the first thing I expect to see when I walk into a professional setting." End of conversation. Hopefully, I upheld the receptionist's dignity and the dignity of her body while at the same time conveying the need for appropriate dress.

This conversion of heart and sight also has transformed my encounters with the naked body in art. While visiting the famous Prado Museum in Madrid, Spain, I tried to visually receive the naked body as God's masterpiece portrayed through its softness, curves, virility, and strength. In trying to see the human body with sacramental sight, I have changed from being judgmental and offended to more prayerful and thoughtful.

God is a Lover and Salvation is Spousal

Interestingly, there is a flip side to cultivating sacramental sight and a sacramental worldview: a new sense of personal censorship. If my senses are designed by God to lead me to Him, then everything I watch, listen to, see, and read needs to be evaluated by this standard. Movies, television, pop music, and current fashions often fall far short in this category.

Once again, the monastery option looks pretty appealing, but the Theology of the Body led me to a different route: I brought the monastery to me. For two years, I have lived deliriously content without a TV in my home. Generally, I watch only "G" or "PG" movies, listen primarily to contemporary Christian music, and delight in dressing in a feminine yet modest way. The result is that my senses are active, alive, and free—free to soak in sensory stimulation without cringing or constantly filtering out what destroys a sacramental sensitivity.

Of course, I don't live in a sacramental bubble: I am still exposed to vulgar language, cohabitating couples, homosexual relationships, hip-hop music at the gym, and billboards, magazines covers, and Super Bowl commercials that objectify the body. However, these remain an exception to the rule and a constant reminder to labor, pray, and have compassion for a culture that has not yet discovered the liberating message of the Theology of the Body, the true meaning of the body, or a sacramental worldview.

While the Holy Spirit is indeed working diligently to transform my daily encounters with the physical world, my spiritual life hasn't been neglected either. Ten years ago, I might have waffled about defending the Real Presence of Christ in the Eucharist. Now I would die for it.

Interestingly, it all comes back to the body. The Eucharist is the sacramental presence of Christ's body here on earth; it is his total and irrevocable gift of self to us. John Paul II says: "The gift given by God to man in Christ is a 'total' or 'radical' gift ... it is in some sense 'all' that God 'could' give of himself to man, considering the limited faculties of man as a creature." I never tire of reading this quote and meditating on it. Imagine ... God, the infinite God, has given all that He could give of Himself to us, considering our limited capacity. He has given Himself to us on the cross and especially in the Eucharist.

At every Mass, God becomes bread so that He can remain "with us always," so that He can be united to us as Lover to lover.

Once again, forget the old man in the sky and the dove! God is a Lover. He is the Bridegroom offering the total gift of Himself to His bride, to *me*. The "great mystery" is that I am invited to become one with God in a way that surpasses marital union. Talk about rocking my world! Especially in light of the deep wound I experienced through my failed earthly marriage, the bridal part of my feminine identity had been completely dismantled.

While I could accept God as Lord, Master, and Savior, it never crossed my mind that He could be my Spouse. That was only for religious and ultra-holy mystics. Yet, in his reflections on Ephesians 5, John Paul II reminds us that Christ's gift of self is a spousal gift destined for each person: "Thus, St. Paul ... shows how the 'Redeemer" ... reveals at the same time that his *saving love*, which consists in his gift of self for the Church, *is a spousal love by which he marries the Church* and makes her his own Body" (TOB 95:7; audience of September 22, 1982).

What remains a mystery to me today—as well as an undeniable truth—is that God invited me into this spousal relationship with Himself through pain and suffering. Mercifully (although it didn't feel like it at the time!), God used pain and loss to detach me from what I tightly clung to as more important than Him, not the least of which was earthly romance. In the process, he created a bridal space within me where divine "holy communion" could be consummated. My body took on another sacred dimension completely unimaginable to me before. It became the place of the most intimate union that two people can share—the one-flesh union—only this one-flesh union was between God and me.

Gradually, as God kneaded these bridal truths into my being (not just my intellect), my understanding of faith and salvation became woefully inadequate. I had always viewed salvation as being "safe"—safe from the fires of hell, safe from God's wrath. While this aspect is indeed true, it is only half the story (it is amazing how many half-truths I lived by without even knowing it!). While we are indeed saved from sin, we are saved for spousal union with God. Salvation is not just a safe event; it is a spousal event!

As this truth penetrates every bit of DNA in my chromosomes, my entire history from conception to eternity has been realigned to express one unabashed truth: I was created for spousal union with God from my conception; I am created for spousal union with God at this moment in my history; and by grace and the cooperation of my free will, I am created for spousal union with God for all eternity in both body and spirit.

Thank goodness my Platonic view of the world and the body was shattered! Thank goodness God didn't allow me to live only half the story for the rest of my life. And thank goodness for Pope John Paul II, who changed my understanding of the body from an optional "extra" to the most precious physical reality on this earth —a sacramental sign of God's presence here on earth.

As *Gaudium et Spes* says, "Man . . . cannot fully find himself except through a sincere gift of himself" (GS, 24). To that I say, "Amen!" and thank you, God, for this body, because I will never be able to fully find myself and my vocation to image a Trinitarian God without it.

Katrina J. Zeno is coordinator of the John Paul II Resource Center for Theology of the Body and Culture for the Diocese of Phoenix. She is also the author of Every Woman's Journey, *reflections on a woman's identity through the lens of the Theology of the Body, and* The Body Reveals God: A Guided Study of Pope John Paul II's Theology of the Body. *Additionally, Katrina is the co-foundress of Women of the Third Millennium, through which she speaks nationally and internationally on the Theology of the Body and Catholic spirituality. Along with Christopher West, she is the co-editor and contributing author to Ascension Press' Theology of the Body pamphlet series. Katrina has hosted or co-hosted several series on EWTN and Catholic Familyland TV. Katrina received her bachelor's degree in theology from Franciscan University of Steubenville, and she is the blessed mother of a young-adult son, Michael. Her web site is www.wttm.org.*

On the Road to Freedom

Steve Pokorny

When many people hear the phrase "Theology of the Body" for the first time, it strikes them as a little strange. They ask, "What does the body have to do with theology?" Commentators on John Paul II's revolutionary catechesis on human sexuality respond, "Everything!"—to which I reply with a resounding heart and voice, "Thank God!"

The aspect of this teaching that resonates most with me is the reality that God actually became flesh and dwelt among us in the person of Jesus Christ. Jesus did not simply give us a good example to follow. Instead, by becoming man—and by loving, living, and dying as a man—He transformed human nature from within. By our entrance into His passion, death, resurrection, and ascension through the sacramental life of the Church, we become empowered with the ability to love as He loves.

For many, even those who consider themselves "good Christians," this sounds impossible. How could we possibly love as Christ loves? Granted, this journey will take a lifetime; even the holiest of saints had imperfections to work out. Yet in a world that advocates the mediocre path, claiming that Christian holiness is a pipe dream, the Theology of the Body makes the bold proclamation that not only is Christ-like love possible; it is essential if we are to fulfill the meaning of our existence. This great hope has sustained me in my most difficult moments of darkness.

Despite the fact that I now dedicate my life to passing on this teaching, the road toward reclaiming the truth about my body and sexuality has been long and hard at times. I am still on the journey, but the road gets smoother everyday.

When I was growing up, I never discussed sex with my parents. In elementary school, I remember doing *Mad Libs* with one of my friends, filling in all the blanks with sexually explicit words. My mom caught onto what we were doing, and she sat me down to have a little chat. "Do you know what sex is?" she asked. "Sure," I answered. That was the extent of the conversation. It was obvious that she was uncomfortable talking about the subject. How different my path might have been had she been able to articulate something of the glorious splendor and God-given purpose of human sexuality—how much pain and agony I could have been spared!

Losing Dad – Twice

I was born into a stable, two-parent home with an older brother, Brian. In 1985, when I was five years old, my life changed. My father, a veteran of the Vietnam War with a get-rich-quick mentality, wagered our house on the stock market without my mom's permission—and he lost. Granted, my father simply wanted to provide for his family. But he had forgotten the essential truth that the dignity of each human person is not found in *what we do* but in *who we are*. We are the beloved sons and daughters of a God who loves us, regardless of our earthly success.

Acting upon the faulty notion that our family needed financial support more than his physical presence, my father believed it would be better to kill himself than to lose the house. He went into the garage, closed the door, and turned on the car in an attempt to end his life. When my mother found him thirty minutes later and dragged him out of the garage, he was alive but his short-term memory would be gone forever due to carbon monoxide poisoning. Because my father was a veteran, the family was taken care of financially. Thus, in a sad twist of irony, my father's fears for a bleak future never came to pass.

My father's condition prevented me from knowing him well. After the accident, he was put in a nursing home and I would occasionally visit him. It was always an uncomfortable situation, for his speech had been slowed and I could not share my experiences of growing older, as he was unable to retain anything that I told him. He was not the father who had played baseball with me in the front yard. Here now was a man who had sold out to his fears and compromised the future of his family. He had destroyed the possibility of our living the "American dream," including my being raised by both a father and a mother.

Because of this abandonment, I grew up insecure and questioned the point of everything. I was often depressed and even felt at times that it would be better if I had never been born. I remember writing more than a few times in my journal that I should kill myself. Despite much counseling, I could not shake the deep-seated depression that gripped my soul.

Much time passed, and around Christmas of 1996, when I was seventeen, my father, at age fifty-one, began to lose a lot of weight. After running tests, the doctors discovered that he had developed brain and lung cancer. He did not have much time left. Within two months he was moved to the Hospice of the Western Reserve in Cleveland. I knew that I had to say something to him before it was too late.

During one of my few visits to hospice, I sat down and was real with him. "You abandoned me, Dad," I said. "You walked out on Mom and Brian. You were not there when we needed you most." For a brief moment, he looked intensely into my eyes and said, "I know." That was his way of saying, "I'm sorry." From that time on, I was able to begin forgiving him. Two weeks later, with our family gathered around his bed, I lost my father for the second time.

The Beginning of the Obsession

When I was in seventh grade, the absence of a father became especially damaging. One day, a friend of mine invited me to his house, and we decided to watch TV. What I saw that day changed me for the rest of my life. He introduced me to hard-core pornography. Although I had been introduced to soft-core porn in the fourth grade through the pages of that year's *Sports Illustrated* Swimsuit Edition and a bag of ripped-up pictures of naked women that I had found on my street, the images on TV that day were much worse.

I began to experience mixed emotions. On the one hand, I was excited and wanted to keep watching; on the other, I had intense feelings of guilt. The more I watched, the uglier I felt. A scene from the movie *A Bug's Life* captures how those pornographic images affected me that day. In the movie, two mosquitoes are hanging out near a bug zapper. The first mosquito says "Frank, get away from the light!" Frank responds, "I can't help it —the light is sooo beauuuuuutiful!" and then . . . ZAAAPP! Frank becomes bug juice. As "beautiful" as I thought the images were, they trapped my soul for more than a decade.

Experts tell us that pornography is the crack-cocaine of sexual addictions. As Lorraine Bennett states, this "erotic haze ... is said to be thirty times more powerful than cocaine."[1] An image can be emblazoned on one's mind in three-tenths of a second and remain there for the rest of one's life unless one experiences a grace-filled healing. Unlike a drug that requires one to take a physical substance into one's body to experience a high, a person who uses pornography simply has to *recall* the image for it to have a stimulatory effect. Like a drug addiction, a pornography addiction often becomes progressive. The user needs new and more dramatic images to give the "kick" he or she seeks.

The effect is similar to Gollum's experience in *The Lord of the Rings*. Gollum's entire life becomes consumed with trying to attain a ring that he believes gives him power. In reality, he is trading his freedom for slavery. The ring is his addiction, and whenever he sees it, the ring's magnetic pull makes his eyes begin to glaze over. A fierce bellow arises from his soul: "My precious!" This pursuit dominates his every thought, and he will do anything to attain the ring, even going so far as to rip it from his brother's cold, dead fingers. However, when he possesses the ring, he feels emptier and lonelier than ever, hating the very thing that he thought would bring him happiness. He is enslaved, with no way out.

Pornography is very much like the ring. For many men, it becomes an all-consuming passion, a world of fantasy that soon enslaves them. This "precious" causes many to lose their jobs, wives, and families. They trade the communion of persons for an absence of community. Thanks to easy access to pornography through the Internet, tens of millions of men have fallen prey to this insidious plague.

---

[1] Lorraine Bennett, "The Secret Sin," Catholic Exchange.com; accessed 5/10/07.

Because of our particular attraction to the visual, men are particularly susceptible to the allure of porn. However, researcher Jason Collum reported that one in six women now struggle with pornography. Neilsen NetRatings reports that thirty-three percent of the users of Internet porn are female.[2] Our culture has been sold the lie that to be intimate, we must act out sexually. Women today seem so thirsty for love that they not only reduce themselves to the level of an object and pose for pornographic publications, but also enter into the world of visually stimulating porn.

The "pornified" culture delivers doses of spiritual arsenic to women. Pornography causes them to look down on their bodies, leading many to believe that if they are to find love, they must live up to the unattainable "sexiness" of airbrushed models found on the covers of supermarket publications. This misperception often leads them to try to dull their internal pain through eating disorders, cutting, and substance abuse.

On another level, a more insidious attack upon women is taking place. Fundamental to the genius of woman is her interiority. A woman is generally more emotionally in tune with others than a man and is able to respond out of this strength. In being rewired through intense visual stimulation, women may lose their more gentle nature and exhibit the more aggressive traits of men. If women begin acting like broken men, the relationship between men and women will break down, making it very difficult for them to become authentic gifts to each other—and thus never fulfill the meaning of their being and existence.

---

[2] Jason Collum, "Obscenity Addictions: A Woman's Struggle, Too," www.CatholicExchange.com; accessed 3/23/04.

I did not have a strong male role model who addressed my coming-of-age issues, and as a result, I did not know how to view women. I came to see women as objects to be used, abused, and discarded. Needless to say, I was uncomfortable being around them. I also found myself disposed to blame women. Just as Adam blamed "the woman" immediately after the Fall, I looked on women with disdain due to their beauty, blaming them for "doing this to me." As much as I wanted to believe that my lusts were their fault, the accusations weighed heavier upon my soul.

You Can Check Out but You Can Never Leave

Because my mom raised me Catholic, I came to understand that the guilt I was feeling was because of my sinful choices, so I went to the sacrament of confession. However, because I did not have a correct understanding of my own sexuality, my life became entrenched in a vicious cycle of abuse. A typical week for me would go like this: I would be tempted, look at pornography, masturbate, feel guilty, go to confession, feel freedom for a few days, and then like Frank's mosquito friend, be drawn back into the dangerous light.

A line in the classic '70s Eagles song *Hotel California* hints at the trap of images in which I found myself after viewing porn: "You can check out any time you like, but you can never leave." Whenever I tried to stop watching pornography, it was as though I were not in full possession of myself. I was like someone who plays video games all day and, when he tries to fall asleep, cannot escape the images to which he has exposed himself.

The situation grew worse. For two years, I experienced emotional shutdown. I lived a kind of "flatline" existence, feeling neither lows nor highs, except during fleeting moments when I indulged in porn. At the age of eighteen, when I should have been spreading my wings and setting out on my life's course, I was wandering in a malaise. Pornography had neutered my spirit. All that was present was a dull ache in my heart, a hurt that could not be mended. I had a self-inflicted, gaping wound that I did not know how to heal.

In high school and then in college, I occasionally sought help. In addition to confession, I would attend Mass and receive the Eucharist in an attempt to feel closer to God. I would go to spiritual direction to bring structure to my disordered life. During my freshman year at Syracuse University, I sensed that I was being called to the priesthood and entered a college seminary. During my time there, several other seminarians and I would try to hold each other accountable, but our best attempts ended in failure. I told myself that this was my cross and that I would have to carry it for the rest of my life. I thought that I would never be free.

Eventually, I realized that pixilated images of women would never satisfy the deep ache within me, but just knowing this information was only one part of the battle. I needed to have a radical heart transplant to be set free to love—but that would not take place for a while.

After three years of college seminary and one year of theological studies in Cleveland, I discerned that God had not given me the gift of celibacy and that I was being called to pursue other paths. He had other plans for me, but a turning point—in my life and in my heart—would be needed if I were to fulfill what He had destined for me before the world began. The prophet Jeremiah explained that God's plan for us is one of life, not death—a plan "for welfare and not for evil" (Jeremiah 29:11). The lifeline God sent came in the form of a tape that my friend Ellen gave me in the summer of 2002. "Just listen to it," she said. Thinking it was another tape on apologetics, I put it in the pile of such tapes that I had accumulated.

A Life Like No Other

As I was getting ready for work one morning during a brutal year of high school teaching in October 2002, I popped in the tape. It was a presentation by Catholic theologian and author Christopher West. I listened to him explain about the human person and the gift of sexuality, and my jaw hit the floor. I realized that this vision of life—this understanding of what it meant to be male and female—was everything for which I was searching!

Christopher's unveiling of God's glorious plan for our lives brought about a mixture of emotions. On the one hand, I experienced great hope, realizing I was not abandoned in my struggle for sexual purity. On the other, I felt a deep pain because I was so far from where I needed to be and had no plan to break free from the chains that bound me. I could relate intimately to the words of St. Paul, "I do not understand my own actions. For I do not do what I want, but I do the very thing I hate" (Romans 7:15). My body and soul were crying out, "How long, O Lord?"

A year later, I began graduate studies at Franciscan University of Steubenville in Ohio. Little did I know that God had much more than a master's degree in theology in store for me. Franciscan is world-renowned for, among other things, its charismatic prayer services known as Festival of Praises. At my first service, it became apparent that God was beginning His work in me in a profound way. One of the Scripture verses proclaimed several times that night was Isaiah

43:19, "Behold, I am doing a new thing; now it springs forth, do you not perceive it?" Through a crack in my stony heart, living waters were beginning to bubble up.

Like many students on campus, I attended daily Mass, where things began getting a little weird—in the best sense of the word. It seemed that the message of virtually every hymn and praise song was directed at me. God was trying to break through my darkness with His glorious, blinding light to allow me to see the truth of His deep love for me. He was wooing me as a bridegroom woos His bride.[3]

Over the course of two weeks, Jesus met me powerfully in the Eucharist. Through the reception of this most holy sacrament, I was being infused with the love of God in a way that I had never experienced. Although I had grown in my relationship with God throughout high school and college, He was introducing me to His most personal and intimate love.

Finding the Father

Once, shortly after receiving the Eucharist, I experienced an intense moment of gratitude for what God was doing with my life. And then it hit me. It wasn't simply Jesus who was moving me to gratitude. It was God *the Father*. This was the Father I had longed for. This union with God—my origin and my destiny—was what I had been looking for in all of those empty pornographic images. The One who I thought had abandoned me had not rejected me but

---

[3] As God is the initiator of the gift of grace, we can use, analogously, such bride-bridegroom language. As human beings, created male and female, we are receptive in relation to Him, even while we fully maintain our masculine or feminine integrity. God was inspiring in me a new gratitude for all that He had done for me.

desired to bring me close and tell me that He loved me far beyond what I could imagine. He had always wanted to hold me and tell me I was His own.

At that moment, I knew I had a Father, a Father who wanted me more than anything. The Greek word used for such an intimate description of God is "Abba," which can be translated as "Daddy." My Abba was calling me to climb into His lap and be held. It was enough. All the fears that I had held inside, all the hurt, all the forgiveness that I couldn't bring myself to accept was washed away by a love that penetrated the deepest core of my being. The floodgates opened and I sobbed like the prodigal son in the arms of his father.

Just when I thought my cup was overflowing with too much love, it happened. I experienced a tangible, potent sense of freedom. For the first time in my life, I knew I was free from my sexual addiction. Just as St. Augustine was liberated from his bonds of slavery to sin when he read the words of St. Paul, "Put on the Lord Jesus Christ, and make no provision for the flesh" (Romans 13:14), I no longer desired to look at sexually explicit images. I had been set *free*. He had brought me to such beauty that pornography failed to contain, namely, Himself. The false way in which I had been seeing women had been replaced by a desire to *serve* the women in my life with humility and to love them as my sisters in Christ.

How did this transformation happen? How did it come to be that I would ever be telling this story of my addiction to pornography? For years, I had lived with the fear, "Don't ever let anyone find out about this addiction or you'll be ruined." But I didn't have to fear anymore. The clouds of darkness in my life dissipated, and I heard in my heart the voice that I had longed to hear, "This is my well-beloved son in whom I am well pleased" (Matthew 3:17). Although this verse is about Jesus, I came to see myself as a son in whom God the Father was well pleased. The destructive vision of self that dominated much of my youth had given way to the "new thing" God was doing in my life.

Satan wants us to think that we are not good enough, that we can never be worthy of our Father's love. He wants us to believe that if we come from broken homes, if we have run away too many times, we are through. The devil wants to immobilize us and keep us locked in our woundedness. But he is wrong—dead wrong. It is not that we are too bad. It is that we are too good—too good to be left alone. God never tires of us. The truth is that He can't get enough of us. That's why the Father sent His Son, and that's the only reason why Jesus' death makes any sense. God loves us so much that He'd rather die than be without us.

Attacking the Root of the Problem

There are many approaches to fighting addictions, but none of them will solve the problem. These strategies are often "sin management," as Christopher West has often pointed out. Unless we attack the root of the issue by allowing the Father to infuse us with His radical grace, we will either continue to struggle or give up because the pain is too much. True, it is good to take precautions and seek assistance, especially in confession, but the key to being healed from any addiction lies not in "doing" things, but in "coming to know" the Father's love. That's the secret. I do not mean to detract from the power of the sacrament; God definitely was preparing my heart to receive His gift of love. However, if we are merely doing things and not opening our hearts to receive what He has in store for us, we will not be set free from our brokenness.

Christ Himself said, "Unless you turn and become like children, you will never enter the kingdom of heaven" (Matthew 18:3). Most of us have sold out to a big lie. We are told to be hard and avoid our emotions, but the love of our Father is totally different. God's love is not a sentimental, fluffy, *Lifetime* television kind of love. It is a love that goes beyond the hardness of this world, a love that gives us the strength to go on when life seems unbearable.

We have to receive this love and know in our hearts that we are loved by our Father. If we are going to complete the work of Christ, we must remember that we can give only what we have. Christ was able to walk on water, perform miracles, give us the Eucharist, and stay on the cross because he knew that His Father *loved Him.* There was no question in His mind that His Father, His Abba, was right there, guiding Him with His love.

Everything I experienced in coming to know the healing love of Christ has been confirmed through my study of Theology of the Body. One of the main points that John Paul elucidates is that, in the beginning, Adam and Eve had the divine vision. With this vision, Adam perceived the interior truth of who Eve was and how he was called to see her. He saw her with the love of her Father, recognizing both her physical body *and* her soul. In seeing Eve's naked body, Adam did not stop at the parts that differentiated her from him, but he saw her *as a person.* In exclaiming, "This at last is bone of my bones and flesh of my flesh" (Genesis 2:23), he was really expressing, "Here is a person that I can love!" Adam voices the desire of every man, who, in his heart of hearts, does not want to use woman but wants to love her with a total gift of himself, laying down his life for her if necessary.

In seeing Eve's naked body and his together, Adam knew that he was called to form a family, or a communion of persons, with his wife. But even more, he knew that in this union, he would be imaging the ultimate Family, the Trinity. He was now able to fulfill the reason for his existence, living as a total-self gift to his bride. Through their fruitful union, Adam and Eve brought forth the greatest gift ever, another unrepeatable human being. Like God, Adam saw how good this was and his heart was at peace.

Although sin causes us to lose this vision, we are not abandoned. By His sacrifice on the cross, Christ redeems our life from destruction and calls us to share in His own divine life. By entering into the Church and continually drawing on the grace of God found in the sacraments, we are able to reclaim this vision and see each other as God sees us. And what is more: Christ empowers us men to love as He loves the Church, offering up our own lives for the women we see so that they may have life, and have it to the full (see John 10:10).

Every man is called to image the Father, to guide others to the heart of Christ. A man without vision cannot lead, for he will simply be a blind man leading the blind. We must recover the divine vision if our society is going to survive, for pornography is destroying the family, the "fundamental cell of society" (see *Familiaris Consortio*, 86). Nakedness is not simply meant for our pleasure; yet, if we learn to see "God's eyes," we can filter out pornography's lies and distortions to see the human body as a revelation of the very mystery of God.

And the best news: It is possible! By the grace of God, I boldly exclaim: I AM A WITNESS TO THIS HOPE! The genuine freedom that I experienced and the renewal that I received are not the exceptions to the rule; they can be the norm for all men. We have to believe this liberation is possible and allow our Father to come into even the darkest corner of our hearts. By coming to know our Father in an intimate way, we will be able to see and experience the full truth of love, something that the false "beauty" of pornography can never capture.

Sharing the Message

Moved by the gift of love poured out on me and by the freedom I had experienced, I wanted to share this message of true sexual freedom with the world. I wrote to Christopher West, sharing with him this good news and asking him what sacrifices I had to make to do what he does for a living. Christopher's encouragement spurred me to action. Over the next few years, I proceeded to work my way through the Theology of the Body and related materials. I have been blessed to study at the Theology of the Body Institute twice, and I have begun an organization, TOB Ministries, devoted to spreading this life-changing message through speaking and writing to anyone willing to listen. By God's grace, I hope to spend the rest of my days proclaiming this life-changing teaching.

Despite the extraordinary healing I have experienced, I wish I could say that I have had no problems since. At times, I have felt the "pull of the flesh" and have slipped, allowing lust to grip my heart.

The truth is that when a person experiences great healing, it enables him to love in a greater way because his chains have been broken. But, in freedom, he still has the ability to say no to God. He can return to the septic tank from which he once drank. But our

God is gracious, patient, and generous. His work in me is far from complete, but He remains near.

My years of pornographic abuse caused me to block my emotions to keep my pain at bay. For years, a deep sadness marked my face, so much so that I could physically feel it, yet I could not figure out why it did. By the grace of God, it was revealed to me about two years ago that I had many layers of shame to strip away.

With God, all things are possible; the fullness of His mercy is ever-present. Through my work with Theophostic Prayer Ministry, a mind-renewal prayer ministry that gets to the root of our wounds; trauma therapy, which has healed my past memories; and meditating on sacred art, the antidote to pornography, I have experienced genuine and lasting freedom from shame—and the power of that pornography once held sway over my heart is firmly broken. Furthermore, I have come to a place of deep peace with my relationship with my earthly father, being able to forgive him completely. Most importantly, I am growing more and more secure in my love of God the Father. He has been setting me free more and more from my self-inflicted crosses, helping me to *know* the freedom of the children of God (see Romans 8:21). This heart knowledge assures me that "I can do all things through in him who strengthens me" (Philippians 4:13).

As I reclaim my masculinity and learn to live in freedom, I plan to continue speaking and writing on the Theology of the Body. By the grace of God, I hope to establish a men's ministry to help men break their bondage to pornography. Many good men are blind to the authentic beauty of women—and Satan desires to keep them in darkness. Because he neutralizes these men, women and children become easy targets. It is my hope that if men can reclaim the meaning of their masculinity and pledge their sacred honor to the dignity of all women and children in their lives, we will see the culture of life blossom in the world.

At World Youth Day in Toronto in 2002, John Paul II said: "We are not a sum total of our mistakes and failures. We are the sum total of our Father's love for us." I have come to know that our Father does not see me as a mistake, but as one who has been endowed with a great grace to love as Christ loves His Church. It is this love that motivates and empowers me to strive to be a gift to others, and I pray that I may be able to impart this hope, that a redeemed sexuality is not some pipe dream but a genuine possibility—and the destiny to which we are called May God be glorified through my woundedness to effect great healing in men and women on their journey to true freedom.

Steve Pokorny is the founder and director of TOB Ministries, an apostolate devoted to the work of fulfilling John Paul II's dream of seeing the culture of life blossom into reality. Steve holds a master's degree in theology from Franciscan University of Steubenville and is currently in the MTS program at the John Paul II Institute for Marriage and Family in Washington, DC. Steve also serves as the coordinator of Catholic Exchange's Theology of the Body channel. For more information about Steve and his work promoting the Theology of the Body, visit www.TOBMinistries.com.

More Than I Could Ask For or Imagine

Anastasia Northrop

"Man cannot live without love. He remains a being that is incomprehensible for himself, his life is senseless, if love is not revealed to him, if he does not encounter love, if he does not experience it and make it his own, if he does not participate intimately in it"
— John Paul II, *Redemptor Hominis, 10*

So began my presentation to the auxiliary bishop, seminarians, twenty Missionaries of Charity, and several hundred others in the hall at London's Westminster Cathedral on September 14, 2006, the feast of the Exaltation of the Cross. When I had first heard of the Theology of the Body seven years earlier, I had no idea I would be dedicating my whole life and work to its dissemination. The truth, however, impels its hearers to dedicate themselves to its proclamation. I also had no idea how the Theology of the Body would help me personally to come to a deeper understanding of the mystery of marriage, the meaning of femininity, and the dignity of the human person. Nor did I foresee how it would transform my relationship with Christ, enrich my life as a single woman, and help me make sense of a toxic dating relationship.

The way I first heard about the Theology of the Body was common enough. In the fall of 1999, a couple of friends mentioned the phrase "theology of the body" to me, and one gave my father an audio tape on the subject by author Christopher West. Even though my family and I produced religious tapes through Our Father's Will Communications, our media apostolate, we rarely listened to any ourselves since we recorded speakers giving talks live all the time. But that day we made an exception. Like many others, we were struck with the power of John Paul II's life-transforming message, and we knew that we wanted to do whatever was possible to spread this message via our media apostolate. Not only did the message convey a deeper understanding of who we are as human persons, but it also had the power to lead us closer to Jesus Christ. Our mission was to evangelize and we quickly realized that this was the perfect way to do it.

In December 1999, we contacted Christopher West to see if we could record him giving a talk or two on the Theology of the Body. Since we were scheduled to record a retreat in California in early January 2000, we asked him if we could stop in Denver to see him on our way back home to the East Coast. We didn't hear back from him for a long while, so as the trip approached we abandoned the idea of any recordings. But twenty minutes before our departure for the long drive across the country, I checked my e-mail, A message from Christopher stated that he happened to be presenting a parish mission in Denver that "would be excellent for us to record" the very week we were heading back home!

It was no coincidence that we ended up recording *Human Sexuality: The Beauty of God's Plan and the Joy of Living It* only sixteen days into the Jubilee Year 2000. Many Theology of the Body promoters credit the grace of this Jubilee Year for the beginning of the spread of the Theology of the Body on a wider, grassroots level. In 2000, sales of Christopher's series *Naked without Shame* (produced by The GIFT Foundation) took off, the first Theology of the Body study group started in Minnesota, the first *Love and Responsibility* study group began in New York, and my family and I, through Our Father's Will Communications, started recording Christopher's talks throughout the United States. That was only the beginning.

In 2001, we moved to Colorado to more easily travel and work with Christopher. Becoming dissatisfied with merely hearing talks about John Paul II's writings on the Theology of the Body, I wanted to read his own words. So a friend and I started a study group in Denver to read and discuss the actual text of the Theology of the Body (retranslated and republished in 2006 as *Man and Woman He Created Them: A Theology of the Body*) with other young adults. I also found it helpful to read John Paul II's earlier foundational book, *Love and Responsibility*. The study group was a great success and one of the highlights of my week. Not only did it facilitate the reading and understanding of the Pope's rich writings, but it also cultivated the *communio personarum* (communion of persons) the he describes. Many relationships were formed and fostered through our weekly discussions, the marriage of my sister and my brother-in-law being just one example. As we read through the text, I gained new insights into how we image God through our sexuality and His plan for the relationship between man and woman. I was also deeply impressed with the idea of "the gift," not only in the sense that the essence of loving is to make a gift of oneself, but with the profound, almost incomprehensible reality of God's gift of His very self to us. As John Paul II said, "God's *gift of himself* to man ... [is] a gift that is in its essential character total (or rather 'radical') and irrevocable ... The freedom of the gift is the response to the deep consciousness of the gift." (TOB 95B:4, 110:9)

Because the study group was such a wonderful experience for my friends and me, I wanted to do whatever I could to encourage others to form similar groups. Between 2003 and 2006, I wrote a study guide for the text of the Theology of the Body entitled *The Freedom of the Gift*. The study guide's summaries, discussion questions, and vocabulary words facilitate the reading of the text both for individuals diving into it on their own and for those who otherwise might have been hesitant to lead a study group.

In my travels recording Theology of the Body presentations by Christopher West and other speakers, such as Katrina Zeno, and through many conversations with Theology of the Body enthusiasts, I began to network with others who were studying and promoting John Paul II's message. In January 2003, thirty-seven of us met in Dallas (home of TOBET, the Theology of the Body Evangelization Team) and formed TOBIA, the Theology of the Body International Alliance, a support network providing resources for people striving to learn and promote John Paul II's understanding of the human person. We brainstormed about how to integrate his beautiful vision into various areas of life and ministry—pro-life work, the media, marriage preparation, singles ministry, youth ministry, street evangelization, and more.

Since then, TOBIA has grown to more than five hundred members in thirty countries and continues to expand. In particular, our National Forum on the Theology of the Body, along with our annual TOBIA gatherings have provided both education about integrating the message and the encouragement and inspiration needed to continue spreading it.[1] In the last six years the various groups and individuals represented

---

[1] These gatherings are open to all. For more information, visit www.tobia.info.

in TOBIA have multiplied as the message of the Theology of the Body has affected hundreds of thousands of lives.

In the latter part of 2004, after hearing speakers Dave Sloan, Katrina Zeno, and Mary Beth Bonacci speak about how to live the Theology of the Body as a single person (not in terms of a permanent vocation, but as a current state in life) I felt called to hold a conference in which singles could hear presentations by all of these speakers. With help from another single friend and the support and encouragement of Dave Sloan, I organized the first National Catholic Singles Conference in Denver in 2005. The conference, which balanced talks, prayer, and social activities, was such a hit that it has become an annual event in multiple locations. The beauty of this conference is that it not only exposes people to John Paul II's liberating message, but it also helps bring singles to an encounter with Jesus Christ, the One who brings healing and freedom and who shows us who we were created to be.

My work has brought me into the orbit of a number of commentators on this extraordinary teaching, including Dr. Philip Mango, Fr. Thomas Loya, and Fr. Roger Landry, among many others, who have helped me to understand how the Theology of the Body can be integrated into every aspect of my life and study. The psychological insights presented by Dr. Mango have been vital to my understanding of the differences between men and women and how they image God differently. Knowing how God created men and women to be complementary and how their needs are different on a practical level has made it easier to understand and appreciate the men in my life. Fr. Loya, with his background as an artist, iconographer, and Eastern Catholic priest, has helped me to understand my own faith and the mystery of God in a way I never have before. Drawing on the riches of

Eastern Christianity, he shows how the spousal imagery can be found throughout the liturgies and prayers of the Church. His explanations on the difference between true art and pornography also have been a great gift to me and countless others. With his keen philosophical and theological insights, Fr. Landry has given me valuable advice for my articles and study guide. Presenting John Paul II's work from different but complementary perspectives, the speakers reveal beautiful facets of the same diamond and show how examining this jewel from all angles enriches everyone.

Over the years, I have come to see how this diamond changes the way one looks at everything. And yet, after having studied, pondered, and taught the Theology of the Body for more than nine years, I know that understanding and integrating it into one's life takes time. This profound teaching certainly provides many "aha" moments, but it takes months or years to really understand the depth of the teaching and effectively apply it to one's daily life. Take, for instance, John Paul's statement, "Purity is the glory of the human body before God. It is God's glory in the human body" (TOB 57:3).

I am the oldest of nine children and grew up with a fairly wholesome understanding of my body. Aside from having the natural insecurities of a teenage girl, I wasn't ashamed of my body or embarrassed about it. After all, in a large family one cannot afford to be. If we had all waited our own turn in the bathroom on Sunday mornings, we never would have made it to church on time! But being comfortable with the human body is not quite the same as being able to see God's glory in the body, or to see God's mystery revealed through it, as John Paul II teaches us we can. Integrating the Theology of the Body is a process, a journey—and knowing the principles contained in it does not automatically guarantee that one will always know how to make the best choices.

Love Can Be Blind…

A few years ago, despite my enthusiasm for the great dignity of the human person, I was still unable to quickly react when that dignity was being trampled in a verbally and emotionally abusive relationship.

As I have learned in the Theology of the Body, we are called to make a gift of self in every aspect of our lives, and aside from the gift of ourselves to God, the most complete gift of our persons we make is in the choice of marriage or consecrated celibacy. In his encyclical *On the Dignity and Vocation of Women (Mulieris Dignitatem)*, John Paul II tells us, "To say that man is created in the image and likeness of God means that man is called to exist 'for' others, to become a gift" (no. 7). As I have learned in the Theology of the Body, we are called to make a gift of self in every aspect of our lives, and aside from the gift of ourselves to God, the most complete gift of our persons we make is in the choice of marriage or consecrated celibacy. As a little girl, I thought, as many little girls naturally think, that I would grow up and meet the handsome prince who would sweep me off my feet. We would get married and live happily ever after. After all, isn't that just what happens? Isn't that what life is all about?

Having had crushes on many guys from the time I was five, I was ready to get married once I hit my twenties. Of course, when my understanding of the beauty of marriage and sexuality was enriched through absorbing the Theology of the Body, I was even more eager to get the show on the road and concretely live in marriage what I had learned. But as many women in my shoes have discovered, it is not as easy as it looks. My mother married at twenty-six. When I was young, I thought that twenty-six was on the older end of the age spectrum. Surely, I thought, I would be married at least by then! I wasn't. My deep desire for marriage—and perhaps also the pictures I had dreamt up about my wedding and life thereafter—contributed to an unpleasant experience with one particular relationship.

At the age of twenty-six, I met Mike[2] at a summer party with other Catholic young adults. He had recently come back to his Catholic faith. Our encounter was brief, and I did not think much of the meeting at the time, but evidently he did. Later in the summer he joined me and several other young adults on a hike. Shortly thereafter, he asked me to dinner. We began to date seriously, and before long we were talking about marriage. Little did I realize that his being "crazy" about me and treating me like a queen was not really as wonderful as it seemed. Having grown up with a healthy family life in which great love and respect were the norm, I was unprepared for the verbal and emotional abuse that followed: jealousy, mistrust, and what I recognized later as efforts to control me. When he first yelled at me and called me names, I was in shock. This was not how I was used to being treated, even in the midst of an argument. Mike said he was sorry for hurting me—even though, according to him, it was my behavior which made him behave in that way.

I knew marriage took work and that relationships were challenging, so it made sense to me that this work would start even before we got married. Being a determined person, I knew I could stick it out. But our arguments increased. He continued to be jealous in spite of my attempts to prove my faithfulness. He insisted that my parents were

---

[2] Name has been changed.

controlling and that I was too attached to my family. He was even jealous of time I spent with girlfriends when he wasn't around. Red flags were popping up all over the place, but I had been praying about the relationship and I thought it was God's will that we work things out, so I kept hanging on.

Because of Mike's negative reactions I did not feel free to share my thoughts and feelings with him. I was afraid of how he might react. I also found myself confused at his childish ultimatums and lack of logic in the midst of our arguments. My efforts to improve the relationship and explain my good intentions did no good. In the end, even if he apologized for hurting me, he still blamed me for his behavior. Of course, he was not always abusive. A lot of the time, he was caring and charming, particularly when we were with other people. That is part of what kept me, and what keeps any woman, going in an unhealthy relationship. We see the good, loving side of the other and continually hope the attractive side will win out and the other side will go away.

Instead of recognizing immediately that Mike was treating me badly and that I shouldn't let anyone speak to me the way he did, I reasoned that we would work things out and the situation would get better. I didn't realize that some situations only get worse with time. Emotional abuse is one of them. As John Paul II said in his book *Love and Responsibility* (published long before he became pope) "What is most essential to love is the affirmation of the value of the person" (p. 183). Emotional abuse is the antithesis of the affirmation of the person; it is an attack on the dignity of the person. Trust is destroyed, freedom is crippled, and the necessary foundations for any real relationship are undermined. Reciprocal love becomes impossible.

Abuse is most often used as a means of controlling another person. Someone who is insecure feels the need to control others to ward off feelings of fear and insecurity. Of course, control leaves no room for what John Paul II called the "freedom of the gift," a freedom that is necessary for love to exist. If love is not free, then it is not love. In reflecting on my relationship with Mike and with other people, I have meditated on this essential point many times.

Our Gift Can Be Our Weakness

Though the break-up was difficult at first, it quickly became more a relief than anything else. I realized that the relationship was not what I wanted my future marriage to look like. It was freeing to be out of the relationship. Only a week after the break-up my dad commented, "It's nice to have the old Anastasia back again." *It's nice to be able to see again*, I thought.

Afterward, I reflected on why and how I had let myself get caught up in that type of relationship and why I had stayed in it for any length of time. Coming from a healthy family and knowing everything I knew about the Theology of the Body, I "should have known better." Or should I have? How did it happen?

Through reading and speaking with others who had experienced abusive relationships, I realized several things. First, unless one has had some experience with controlling and abusive relationships, it is not easy to see one coming. Good Catholic men are not exempt from abusive behavior. Often, the need to control comes from a wounded past. Some men know they are controlling their partners and don't think it's a problem; others may not be aware of the harm they are causing. Either way, they don't act hurtfully all the time. On the contrary, they can be quite charming. A man often tries to make the best impression possible until, through engagement or marriage, he knows he "has" her.

In addition, a woman's natural desire for relationship and her hope for the best can keep her focused on the goodness of the person in the midst of difficult times. Naturally, couples are called to have this perspective throughout the normal struggles of any relationship. I did not realize that the same does not hold true when one is discerning whether to marry a person who doesn't treat others with respect.

Finally, the nature of verbal and emotional abuse is that it eventually causes the woman on the receiving end to doubt her sanity. All those around her think the man she is dating (or married to) is wonderful. She may be the only one who sees his demeaning side. Perhaps it is only her imagination. Perhaps it really is all her fault—and if she just improves this or changes that, things will get better. As women, we are particularly susceptible to being hurt through emotional abuse because it is written into our nature to receive. The "genius" of woman that John Paul II speaks about involves our unique openness to the person and our attention to relationships. When it comes to abuse we are more inclined to receive it and interiorize it. These God-given qualities of woman—to be receptive and reflective—make it easy to fall into and stay in an abusive relationship.

I also realized, especially through my work with the Theology of the Body, that other tendencies we women have also contribute to our remaining in abusive relationships. These tendencies are the result of original sin. One of the reasons why I was in the relationship with Mike was that he was the first man who had ever fallen "head over heels" for me, who treated me like I was the most wonderful woman in the world. Frankly, I liked that. I was taken in by it. God made us women to be loved and to desire love, but sin has distorted that desire and exaggerated it. After sin, God said to Eve, "Your desire will be for your husband, and he will rule over you" (Genesis 3:16). This is not how God created the male-female relationship to be, nor was it a "punishment" he imposed on Adam and Eve. Rather, it was a consequence of their sin. It was something that appeared as a natural result of their actions and was an attitude that they would have to fight against for the rest of their lives—and which we, their descendants, have to combat as well. The root of sin is replacing God with something else, creating an idol. Sin has made it much easier for us to put another person—in my case, the attention of a man—in place of God, often without realizing it.

Trusting More Deeply

As time has passed I have realized that, because on the deepest level I haven't completely believed in God's unconditional love for me, and believed that He finds me, a sinner, beautiful and delightful, I've looked for that affirmation in my relationships with men. Until you believe in the depths of your being in God's overwhelming love for you, you will always look for it elsewhere. And since another person will never be able to satisfy that love, ultimately you will never be fulfilled. When, after much prayer and reflection, God gave me the grace of really knowing in my being that He delights in me as His daughter, I realized that I would no longer be burdening my future husband with expectations he couldn't possibly fulfill. Instead, by accepting and receiving God's love and keeping my eyes on Him as my hope, my love for my future husband and his love for me would be in its proper context, as a reflection of God's love, not as a burden that neither of us would be able to carry.

After my relationship ended, my natural desire to be loved had been distorted to the point that I would put up with "non-love" to keep Mike's attention and affection. Of course, I didn't think of it that way at the time. Only afterward, when I was trying to figure out how I had gotten into the relationship and how I had stayed in it for any length of time, did I see the connection. Mike was not the type of guy I was usually attracted to, nor was he someone who would typically be a close friend. I knew that I wanted to marry my best friend, but somehow I had reached the point at which I was thinking of marrying someone who really wasn't even my friend! I had been blind.

Lastly, I have only recently realized that the relationship had another component. During and after the relationship, my mother commented that she thought I was more in love with the idea of getting married than I was with Mike. *Of course not,* I thought. Five years have passed since our relationship, and I have begun to think she was right. I certainly never thought I would be over thirty and not married. But it happened, and I survived. In my work with singles ministry and the National Catholic Singles Conference, I have had the opportunity to think a lot about marriage and my desire for it. It is not uncommon for women who are in their thirties and forties and who thought they would be married by now to settle for less than a "Theology of the Body relationship." (It is also possible to be too picky and expect to marry a "perfect" man, an utter impossibility unless one is entering a convent with Christ as one's only spouse.) Some people idolize their boyfriend or their spouse. For me, it was not a particular person but the idea of marriage.

Growing up, I was taught to love God above all things and to seek His will at all times. I didn't realize, though, that my desire for marriage was getting in the way of my complete and total surrender to God, my ultimate Spouse. It has taken me a long time to recognize and receive this truth. The more I comprehend His great gift the more I can trust the incredible Love who is that gift.

In Karol Wojtyla's play *The Jeweler's Shop*, the character Adam says to Anna, "Ah, Anna, how am I to prove to you that on the other side of all those loves which fill our lives—there is Love! The Bridegroom is coming down this street and walks every street! How am I to prove to you that you are the bride?"[3] Trusting the love of God as my first Bridegroom is an ongoing process for me, especially with regard to my vocation. Ultimately, I must receive God's unconditional love and respond to it first. Only then will any future relationship with a man have the correct balance and the freedom necessary for the complete gift of self.

If I am to be married, I must remember that the man He has in store for me is entirely a gift. Only through my unreserved surrender to God and radical confidence in Him will I be able to make a free gift of myself to that man, without wanting from him and from our relationship the fulfillment that can be found only in God. This is what true freedom means.

My experience with John Paul II's legacy is not one which caused a radical change in my lifestyle, at least not in how I was living my

---

[3] Karol Wojtyla. *The Jeweler's Shop* (San Francisco, Ignatius, 1992), p. 64.

sexuality. I grew up knowing and living the Church's teaching in that regard. But it has enriched tremendously my understanding of the meaning and beauty of my femininity and of the marriage relationship. It has helped me to understand the roots of sexual morality, the contrast between loving and using another person. It has shown me what it really means to be made in the image and likeness of God, the great dignity that this entails, and what it means to love. Eight years ago, had someone told me that there was a talk going on at my local parish about the Church's teaching on sexuality, I probably wouldn't have gone because I thought I knew it already. Little did I know how deeply John Paul II's beautiful writings would profoundly impact my understanding of what it really means to be a woman. Knowing that my sexuality is meant to drive me to make a gift of myself in all areas of my life is an indispensable tool for living as a single person in today's world. It is invaluable for me to know that I can be a spiritual mother to many, that I can receive and nurture others spiritually and emotionally as I wait on God to direct my life according to His timing, secure in the knowledge that if I am actively seeking His will at all times, He, in his infinite love, will lead me to my vocation in His time.

My "conversion story" is one of ongoing conversion, of progressively dying to self more and more so that I can live in the freedom and the joy that Christ is offering me. The Theology of the Body has been an essential means by which I have been able to enter into that daily conversion more fully and through it to know the "love of Christ which surpasses knowledge," that love "whose power now at work in us can do immeasurably more than we can ask or imagine" (Ephesians 3:19-20).

Anastasia Northrop is president of TOBIA, the Theology of the Body International Alliance. For the past nine years she has worked full time with Our Father's Will Communications in promoting John Paul II's understanding of the human person worldwide. Along with organizing conferences and writing articles related to the theology of the body, she has given talks and promoted study groups in the United States and several other countries in Europe and South America. She is the author of the study guide for the text of the Theology of the Body entitled The Freedom of the Gift. *For resources on the Theology of the Body, more information about TOBIA or to contact Anastasia visit www.TheologyoftheBody.net.*

What's So Funny 'bout Peace, Love, and Embodiment?

My Journey into the Theology of the Body

Glenn T. Stanton

I knew little of him and he knew nothing of me, an anonymous appointment on his packed calendar. Yet, he was gracious to make time.

I heard he could help young authors find the money needed to complete book projects that were languishing due to the demands of day jobs. I was struggling to finish my first book, *Why Marriage Matters*, a project exploring the social sciences for the substantial medical, psychological, and general "well-being benefits" that marriage provides for adults, their children, and society. The book's deadline was staring down the birth of our twins. Not much work was going to get done after these two little ones arrived, so I was searching for money to take time off from work and put this project to bed. Off I went to see this man in Washington, DC.

On the day of our appointment, he invited me into his office. Making introductory small talk, I commented on the gazillion books that filled every inch of his walls, noting that one could get smarter by just sharing the physical space with the all these impressive volumes. He considered the possibility.

While scanning his books, I noted a large, framed photograph of the current pope. It was clear from the placement of this photograph—it was simply hung in the middle of one of the shelves, boldly and carelessly blocking a number of levels of volumes—that the pope held a special place in my host's life and work. Wanting to share my own regard for the man, I commented: "That dude's awesome." He politely replied that yes, this gentleman was certainly an individual of significant consequence.

We took seats and moved onto our business. After I offered my plea, it turned out that he was not in the business of giving money, but he offered to write to some potential sources on my behalf and also recommend some publishers. We shook hands and I thanked him for his time, advice, and graciousness. He followed up on his promise, and I finished the book days before our twins entered the world, even without my having secured the extra financial support.

It was only after I had learned that Pope John Paul II had selected an unofficial "official" biographer that I discovered who this kind kibitzer really was. And to think that I had referred to John Paul the Great as "that dude" right there in George Weigel's office just when he was surely starting work on his biographical feat! One can feel crippling embarrassment over an event years after the offense.

Many years later, I went on a road trip to visit friends. As I passed through the beautiful hill country of Charlottesville, Virginia, on a crisp autumn morning, I listened to a radio interview with this George Weigel, who was discussing his authoritative biography on John Paul II. My ears perked up when he started talking about a particularly important teaching John Paul II had given at the beginning of his pontificate called the Theology of the Body.

Weigel made two points about this teaching.

First, this body of work was both intellectually sophisticated and substantively dense. I took note of that as a challenge. I had done my graduate work in philosophy and was attracted to these ideas in the way a climber would be attracted to Mount Everest or a businessman to a challenging enterprise. Second, this teaching was a brilliant repudiation of so-called Gnostic Christianity. That grabbed me by the throat.

For several years, I had been working with a Christian gentleman who had taught me more about spirituality than nearly anyone had up to this time. When I tell people about him, they usually reply, "Isn't it nice when God gives you such a gift?"

It wasn't like that. This man was no gift. He rubbed me raw at nearly every turn. But our faith teaches that such burdens *can* bear good fruit, and this one did.

He was a nice enough man, usually kind, deeply committed to his faith, a good father, and a conscientious citizen, but he lived in a world so black and white it would make a Dalmatian look like a Technicolor beast. He had no use for any mystery in God or nuance in life. Unbeknownst to him, he had God on a pretty short leash. This was his spirituality. In my view, he was not really a Christian but an unwitting Platonist, seeing all value in the spiritual and nothing good in the physical. We butted heads constantly, and I grew to despise his brand of spirituality— especially his arrogance masked as spiritual conviction and his pathetically small view of God and creation. Unfortunately, I saw this same type of subtle Platonism in many of my evangelical brothers and sisters. I knew Christianity had a larger view of God, humanity, and creation.

On the back roads of Virginia that morning, I found in Weigel's explanation of the Theology of the Body something I wanted to explore, something I desperately *needed* to explore, as a way to illuminate a spirituality that was markedly different from my colleague's. This was an answer to the small but serious crisis of faith through which I was stumbling. Perhaps it was more of a crisis of discipleship, for I had doubts not about my Christian faith but about how my fellow sojourners and I practiced it. I knew that our historic faith was much more robust, profound, and beautiful than what we were daily snacking on and living out. If it was worth the name, then our Christianity had to be as large as its founder, the King of glory and of creation. A good person to look to for this larger, fuller understanding seemed to be the man who gave the world this Theology of the Body.

Diving into the Depths

Additionally—and I am not sure where I got this idea—I knew I had to learn more about "that dude" whose life Weigel had chronicled and about the truths he proclaimed, even if he happened to be "one of those Catholics."

I asked for Weigel's biography, *Witness to Hope,* and on Christmas morning 2000, I found the massive volume, a gift from my wife, under our tree. Immediately, I started reading and encountered the incredible life story of Karol Wojtyla: beautiful scholar, creative actor, gifted poet and playwright, groundbreaking theologian, active sportsman and outdoorsman, loving and natural pastor, cunning political resistant, and human rights activist. In all these roles, this man had a quiet, natural hipness. The only thing lacking was that he didn't play jazz.

After Weigel's incredible introduction, I eagerly went to other volumes to explore not only the Theology of the Body but also the larger philosophy behind it. My first stop was Rocco Buttiglione's intellectual biography, *Karol Wojtyla: The Thought of the Man Who Became Pope John Paul II*, which helped me to understand how this pope grew to be such an intellectual and theological giant. This new material in phenomenology and personalism was like a pint of Guinness: thick, difficult to see any light through, and an acquired taste. But it also was surprisingly nutritious, fulfilling, and worth the effort. But at this early stage, I went looking for something akin to a Black and Tan to lighten the beverage.

I found help in Fr. Richard Hogan and Fr. John LeVoir's *Covenant of Love*, which begins with a simple biography of John Paul II and moves into a thoughtful explanation of his philosophy of the human person. I cannot overstate the impact this material had on my mind and my soul. Their explanation helped me see how profound Christianity is in answering the deepest questions we all have about who we are, how we relate to others and God's relationship to us. I not only learned about John Paul's philosophy and got answers to my questions, but also realized that the questions I had been asking were inadequate. Far more pressing questions centered on what it means to be human.

As a conservative evangelical, I knew that anyone who tried to teach you how to be an "authentic human-being" was probably some mushy secularist, a Unitarian, or a New Ager. Yet here was the pope directing me to a deeper understanding of who Christ is, the Trinitarian God, and the profound nature of the Incarnation while simultaneously explaining how to be more truly human. In my reaction to the juxtaposition of these ideas, I learned I was more like my colleague than I had realized.

True Christianity and authentic humanism are not opposed. The Christian story of creation, the Fall, the Incarnation, redemption, and the ascension illumines what it means to be human and, ultimately, is what the human body points us to. It is unfortunate that the evangelical worldview emphasizes only the creation, the Fall, and redemption, even though evangelical Christians fully believe in the other two realities.

Of course, to an evangelical, the Lordship of Christ is a foundational tenet. But evangelicals do not fully appreciate this truth. I know I didn't. John Paul II's philosophy helped me see that the Christian system coheres in a more sophisticated way than I had imagined. It brought the physical and spiritual together in a profound way. Christ, the God-man, was not just a theological or metaphysical puzzle. Rather, He brought redemption to both the spiritual and physical parts of life. His Lordship was indeed total, not just in my own life in terms of what I did or didn't do but over *all* of creation and human experience.

A Foreign World

As I reread Weigel's biography today, I am struck by how geographically and ideologically foreign Karol Wojtyla's story was to me then and how familiar it has become in these few intervening years.

As an evangelical, I was trained in the "early church fathers" of Luther and Calvin, not to mention their more recent counterparts: Billy Graham, Carl Henry, and Francis Schaeffer. But John Paul drew from a deeper, more ancient tradition (I can hear my good Catholic friends cackling too loudly here). I do believe he will be remembered as the third great Christian theological "systematizer," following Augustine and Aquinas. His work will take centuries to unpack and apply.

John Paul II gives the world a new way of understanding Christian truth based on a brilliant and faithful illumination of Scripture, leading to a new application of the philosophical systems of phenomenology and personalism. At first, it was all so strange and different. For example, he discussed subjectivism (a view that emphasizes personal experience as a means to knowledge) as a positive—a position that I was not used to. Nevertheless, it had a life-giving hold of me and wouldn't let go.

In the summer of 2007, I was able to visit John Paul's home city of Krakow and see all the sites that had been part of his life: the small apartment that he shared with his father, the nearby parish church where he had served as an altar boy, and the houses of friends in the neighborhood—a neighborhood that bordered Oskar Schindler's. I imagined him bounding out his front door and running around the corner to his friend's house. I stood in front of the archbishop's residence where, more than fifty years earlier, Karol Wojtyla had been ordained a priest. I saw his university, seminary, and the various churches where he served as a priest, as well as Wawel Cathedral, where he served as archbishop of Krakow. All of these sites, which contributed to one of the most consequential lives of the twentieth century, are within walking distance of one another. As a result of this trip, aspects of Wojtyla's early story coalesced and seemed less strange.

In *Witness to Hope*, Weigel gives the searching reader a taste of the atomic nature of the Theology of the Body:

> John Paul's *Theology of the Body* may prove to be the decisive moment in exorcising the Manichean demon and its deprecation of human sexuality from Catholic moral theology.

> Few moral theologians have taken our embodiment as male
> and female as seriously at John Paul II. Few have dared push
> the Catholic sacramental intuition—the invisible manifest
> through the visible, the extraordinary that lies on the far side
> of the ordinary—quite as far as John Paul does in teaching
> that the self-giving love of sexual communion is an icon of the
> interior life of God.[1]

A sentence such as that last one—sex as an icon of the interior life—is mind blowing. And if that connection makes Christian readers uncomfortable, they must read the Theology of the Body, for it is much more than a provocative statement. It speaks deeply about who we are, who God is, and how He seeks to reveal Himself to us in beautiful and profound ways. As Weigel concludes, "Few have dared say so forthrightly to the world, 'Human sexuality is far greater than you imagine.'"[2]

And indeed, this is the profound message of the Theology of the Body. But I will take Weigel's conclusion even further without the slightest concern for overstatement. I think John Paul II's presentation of human sexuality is unparalleled in its beauty and its faithful depiction of who God is and who we are. No one has ever developed a framework for understanding and practicing human sexuality and love that can compare with it. And yes, that includes even the Kama Sutra.

What I Found in the Theology of the Body

John Paul II was a disciple of Christ who faithfully sought to present the timeless, life-giving Gospel to his unique and challenging generation. He did so by showing how our human "body in fact, and only the body, is capable of making visible what is invisible: the spirit

---

[1]   George Weigel, *Witness to Hope* (New York, NY: HarperCollins, 1999), p. 342.
[2]   *Ibid.*, p. 65

and the divine."[3] Not only are our bodies good; they are much more. They are, as we read in Genesis 1, profound symbols or icons of the invisible God. Although everything God created is good, our bodies are the only physical parts of creation that serve as an icon of God.

Let us pretend for a moment that we witnesses to the six days of creation. We hear God proclaim that He wants to make something in His image and likeness (Genesis 1:26). The Creator is going to give the world a physical picture of the invisible God. We wait expectantly to see what this glorious image will be. *What could possibly show forth the image of the eternal, glorious God in the world?* In a creative flash of glory, two beings appear. It is these who are a physical manifestation of God. They are male and female, two different forms of what we know as humanity.

In ways that no other part of creation can or does, these beings physically show forth the image of the invisible God, and that is what each of us, and every other person we encounter, does. This brings a proper understanding of theology and anthropology together in a beautiful and true way. Theism is connected and gives meaning to humanism.

Man in his solitude, as described in the second creation narrative (Genesis 2), did not represent the image of the Trinitarian God, whose essence is community. That is why it was "not good that the man should be alone" (Genesis 2:18). As a God image-bearer, he was not created to be alone. We represent the image of God in relation to another, by seeking to love another as God loves—in His eternal communion as Trinity and toward each of us. John Paul explains:

---

[3]   *Man and Woman He Created Them*, February 20, 1980

Man becomes in image of God not so much in the moment of solitude as in the moment of communion. He is, in fact, "from the beginning" not only an image in which the solitude of one Person, who rules the world, mirrors itself, but also and essentially the image of an inscrutable divine communion of Persons. In this way, the second (Genesis 2 or *Yahwist*) account could also prepare for understanding the trinitarian concept of the "image of God," even if "image" appears only in the first (Genesis I or *Elohist*) account. This is obviously not without significance for the theology of the body, but constitutes perhaps the deepest theological aspect of everything one can say about man.[4]

To me, this statement about humanity is the most profound in all of literature. John Paul II explains that our embodiment as male and female and our communion with the other is how we most significantly exemplify the image of the Trinitarian, communitarian God in our humanity. This statement explains what we are made *for* because of what we are made *from*, why loneliness and exclusion are among the most painful of human experiences, and why even the most hardened criminal is crushed by solitary confinement. It explains why human touch is so powerful and why a child will not fully develop without it. It explains why we will do the craziest things to find the slightest and most artificial bit of human connection, from pornography, to phone sex, to Internet relationships. And it is not all about sex either. Prostitutes through the ages tell of male clients who ask just to be held or listened to. This is why some women develop emotional relationships with men who aren't their husbands. People really do need people—and people need to be needed by people.

---

[4]   *Ibid.*, November 14, 1979

In light of our creation, we relate to others and live out our humanity primarily *through our bodies*—through hearing and speech, through appearance and touch, through just being. This understanding transformed my relationship with Jackie, my wife of twenty years. It transformed our sexual relationship, but not in the ways one might think. It didn't serve as a sex manual, providing helpful tips and techniques. It made our sex life *deeper*. It gave it a much larger context, a more profound meaning. Sex was no longer just fun, romantic, or emotionally fulfilling. It certainly was *all* of those things, but it became more. And this larger context enhanced each of those aspects. It helped us understand what we were really participating in our God-given ability to share ourselves fully with one another. It helped us appreciate how this special union was a bodily, fleshly, and shadowy manifestation of the spiritual intimacy that the Godhead shared from eternity. Our love models God's love in that, by its nature, it must flower in creative power in bringing forth new life. God not only creates new life in new creations—new beings—but also new life in all areas of these new beings. The Gospel is about redeeming and making all things new. Jackie and I participate in this creative activity as humans, as Christians, as spouses, and as parents. With this new understanding and insight, I can no longer look at these expressions of my created humanity casually.

Jackie and I learned that our bodies tell us something about God and His plan to redeem us. The Christian story is the story of the God-man, the second person of the Trinity, embodied in the living, crucified, resurrected, and ascended historical person of Jesus Christ. The Word became—and becomes—flesh. It is why Pope John Paul II, in the first line of his first papal encyclical, *Redemptor Hominis*, boldly and prophetically proclaims, "The Redeemer of Man, Jesus Christ, is the centre of the universe and of history."

I learned that everything—emphasis on the word *every*—revolves around Jesus Christ, God embodied. God comes to earth and dwells among us through the Incarnation. He is crucified and buried, bodily. Human flesh enters heaven in the ascension of the bodily resurrected Christ, the firstborn of those who will rise. Not only does this central Christian truth disprove Gnosticism; it blows it to bits, reconciling the physical and spiritual as no other theological or philosophical system does.

C. S. Lewis, as close a "pope" as we evangelicals have:

> Christianity is almost the only one of the great religions which thoroughly approves of the body—which believes that matter is good, [where] God Himself once took on a human body. ... There is no good trying to be more spiritual than God. God never meant man to be a purely spiritual creature. That is why He uses material things like bread and wine to put the new life into us. We may think this rather crude and unspiritual. God does not: He invented eating. He likes matter. He invented it.[5]

Help in My Day Job

Another reason for my interest in the Theology of the Body is my day job. I went to work at Focus on the Family right after finishing my master's program in philosophy and humanities in the early '90s. I have been there ever since, working as a researcher, speaker, and writer on marriage and parenting issues. I am one of those rare and

---

[5]   C.S. Lewis, *Mere Christianity*

fortunate individuals who does for a living exactly what he would do if money weren't an issue (though I might start my workday a little later in the morning!). I get to study and communicate the sociological, anthropological and theological importance of marriage and family. My prejudice is that I cannot imagine more important work for someone who seeks to apply the truths of God to how we live our human lives.

My primary interest over the last few years, given the direction of our culture is how gender intersects with family in terms of marriage and parenting. Are husbands and wives, mothers and fathers essential to the family and human development? That question is not so obvious to everyone anymore, and the task of the day is to explain why asking it matters more than we can imagine. Our culture is becoming increasingly adrift on the issues of sexual differentiation and gender. I speak on secular college campuses many times a year, debating the issue of same-sex marriage to largely suspicious or openly hostile audiences. Two of the most controversial statements one can make on a college campus today are that men and women are intrinsically different and that humanity is binary. I have been shouted down at many a "free-thinking" university for saying exactly that in the most civil of tones. On one occasion, such radical statements required campus security to escort me safely to my car after speaking at the University of Wisconsin–Madison.

Ideas are dangerous. Today, unfortunately, young people hear "different" as "unequal." I also hear otherwise intelligent students say the wackiest things about gender, making me wonder if a class action suit could be brought against some Gender Studies departments for intellectual malpractice. A young student recently tried to correct my "cluelessness" by explaining that, as far back as the Middle Ages, there were as many as *eight* different genders. I told him with all the patience I could muster that he must be reading Aquinas in the original language, because my simple reading of him revealed nothing of the sort.

Another student told me that males and females only recently started dressing differently and distinguishing themselves in physical presentation. He impressed me with this idea because he confidently went into detail about how tailoring had recently changed to reveal these supposed gender distinctions. I asked him if he were a student of art history. He affirmed that he was. Why then, I asked, could you view art from *any* period, from *any* culture, and not have the slightest problem discerning the male figures from the female, even without the tiniest bit of understanding about their particular fashion ideals? The look of "now, that's a good point" is unmistakable, and this student had it. I also tell my audiences that, for all the proposed rainbow of gender diversity, I have never met anyone in all my campus visits who did not present themselves as either male or female, regardless of what their biology stated. Why don't transgendered folks ever "trans" into anything other than male or female? And these people are supposed to be creative boundary-pushers!

Why Theology of the Body Matters in the Human and Cosmic Battle

Christians should easily discern why gender is such a white-hot issue today. At creation, Satan enticed Adam and Eve to doubt the word of God.

Today, he is taking his bitter jealousy of God a step further. He is enticing many to doubt not just the *word* of God but His very *image* in creation. Satan is doing this by attacking the value of male and female as the unique image-bearers of God in the world. Mere social constructs tell us nothing about the God of the universe and His nature, but intentionally created beings do. Satan is attacking the image of God by defacing the sacred virtue of male and female and the beautiful gift of sexuality. He is attacking the sacred union of marriage by reducing it to a temporary legal contract that is only as strong as our emotional desires. He is attacking the role of parents, through whom God creates and to whom God entrusts the next generation of His image-bearers. Abortion has turned parents into destroyers, making the human contract between parent and child valid only if the mother desires the child.

It is in family that we are most human. And it is at the intersections of all the aspects of family that Satan is working his hardest today. It is no wonder that in the mystery of family—the place where each of us finds our earthly origin—we find the most realistic and profound imaging of the mystery and community of God as Trinity, where all of reality has its origin.

On February 20, 1980, John Paul II told the world in his general audience, "In the mystery of creation, man and woman are a reciprocal gift." And this is a gift given to each other and given to us from God to reveal Himself to us at every place on earth through every person at every moment. We enter the race in only one way: *from* the intense passion, intimacy, and love of the Holy Trinity and *through* the intimacy, love, and warmth of our parents at conception and birth. Scripture and John Paul II's Theology of the Body teach us that this common human experience is more profound than we can imagine. It speaks and connects us to a mystery that is far larger than each of us.

Glenn T. Stanton is the director of global family formation studies at Focus on the Family and a research fellow at the Institut du Mariage et de la Famille Canada in Ottawa, Ontario. He is the author of three books on family, including My Crazy Imperfect Christian Family, *offering a practical theology of family life. He and his wife have five young children and live in Colorado Springs, Colorado.*

From Burden to Blessing

Heather Smith

For many years, I lived my life searching for God's love and buying into any counterfeit love the world offered. Because of my journey in the Theology of the Body, I now know that God wants me to come out of hiding, to share the things that I am most ashamed of, to trust Him, and to be the woman He loves—not because I have "earned" it or am "good enough" but because He has loved me from all eternity. The Theology of the Body has helped me learn what it means to be a daughter, His daughter; my desire is to be an authentic woman, the woman God created me to be.

God has loved me from all eternity. This truth was manifested from the moment that I was conceived. My parents had been married five years, and their chance of having a baby was nearly hopeless. My mother was minutes away from having a medical procedure to help her conceive. However, even with a successful surgery, the possibility of pregnancy was small. Just as she was being wheeled into the operating room, a doctor came in with shocking news. My mother was pregnant! Had this been discovered five minutes later, I would have been destroyed during the procedure. Though I have heard this story since I was a little girl, I have only recently come to understand its deeper message: My parents had wanted me. I was their miracle, and God had protected me. He had fought for me before I even came into the world.

But His words were lost in the wounds of my life. From as early as I can remember, I have lived a life in hiding, shame, fear, and doubt. The oldest of four children, I grew up in a home with an alcoholic father. I always felt as if I weren't his priority—as if I didn't matter to him. I desperately wanted his love and thought I could earn it by being a good and perfect daughter. I thought if I were good enough, he might love me enough to stop drinking. He often tried to stop and would promise never to drink again, but his promises were always broken. After a while, I had little faith in his promises (or anyone else's, for that matter). I prayed to God that He would help my father stop drinking, but when his drinking continued, I felt let down by both of my fathers—my dad and God the Father. Whom could I trust? It seemed as if my whole world would crumble at any moment. I had bought into three damaging lies: prayers were not answered, I could only rely on myself, and being a daughter was painful.

My shame, fear, and desire for love continued in high school. At seventeen, I was still trying to present the perfect image and to please anyone who I thought was someone. I was a model student, and I had been accepted into college. But I was filled with loneliness. My desire to be loved and to please led me to make sexual choices with boyfriends that I would later regret, choices that would fill me with a haunting shame for many years to come. I rationalized my behavior by thinking it was okay because we were "in love," but part of me felt guilty for my actions. I knew that my parents and the Church wanted me to save sex until marriage. But I did not understand why waiting was important. I thought it was just some social convention made up centuries ago and out of step with modern times. As far as I could tell, everyone in my high school was "doing it." But I could not see the deep pain it was causing, even in my own life.

The priest at my parish, Fr. Tom, was someone I respected. He reached out to the high school youth at our church. He took an interest in our lives, and he attended our sporting events and took us out for pizza. Fr. Tom and I had a rapport, but I felt I couldn't possibly share with him the areas of my life in which I was sinning, especially my sexual sins. Ironically, around this time, he asked me to help him start an abstinence program in our parish. I agreed because part of me wanted to know why it was important to live purely. However, deep within my heart, I knew that I was a fraud. To compound my guilt, I found out within the month that I was pregnant. The "love" that had earlier rationalized my behavior evaporated as quickly as most high school crushes. In an instant, all of my goals for my future seemed to disintegrate. These were the darkest days of my life; the shame was paralyzing. I was three months from graduating, with several scholarships on the line, and I was pregnant and alone. My desperation was profound. I had let everyone down.

Confused but Searching

The shame of hiding alcoholism in our family was nothing compared to the despair I felt during my pregnancy. I was terrified to tell Fr. Tom that I wouldn't be working on the abstinence program because I was pregnant. I would have rather died than to be honest with him. Thankfully, God intervened and made this the gentlest encounter. I was at a friend's house when the doorbell rang. When my friend opened the door, Fr. Tom was standing there. "I've been looking for you," he said. Somehow he had learned of my situation. I had been so afraid to face him, yet he had come to me. He said, "I love you and God loves you."

This meant so much to me at the time. I look back and now see that Fr. Tom's love was God's love, his acceptance was God's acceptance.

Several months before finding out I was pregnant, I had listened to a talk on abortion. The speaker, a Catholic, had told us to make up our mind about abortion at that moment, not when we were faced with the actual decision. I decided that night I would never have an abortion. From the day I learned I was pregnant, I knew abortion was not an option. I am so thankful for that woman and for the strength—God's strength—to be obedient to life.

I hid my pregnancy from most people until it became obvious. I couldn't find the words to say I was having a baby. I couldn't figure out how to fake a happy voice, and I wasn't even sure if I was supposed to pretend to be excited.

My parents urged me to go to confession. I finally agreed to go at a neighboring parish to a priest who didn't know me. Entering the confessional was terrifying. I began by mentioning some minor sins and then, with great difficulty, I forced myself to confess the premarital sex. I said it in a whisper, and I'm surprised the priest even heard me. But he responded, "God loves you. That's why he wants you to save sex for marriage. He wants to protect you." It was the first time I had ever heard chastity described in a loving and positive light, yet I still did not understand it. The priest went on to tell me about some of the consequences that God wanted to protect me from, one of them being an out-of-wedlock pregnancy. I didn't have the courage to tell him that I was already pregnant. I think my lack of honesty at that moment compounded the guilt and shame I felt, and, in part, blocked my ability to forgive myself.

Nine months later, I gave birth to a beautiful baby boy. Within four days of giving birth, I returned to my college classes. I didn't celebrate; I just survived. I worked tirelessly, trying to prove that I wouldn't be just another single mother statistic. I deeply yearned to know that I mattered to this world.

Relying on My Own Strength

In addition to feeling guilt and shame for my sin and pregnancy, I also felt completely irresponsible. The messages I had heard from the world were "protect yourself," "have safe sex," and "use contraception." The only difference between what I did and what my friends were doing was that I got pregnant. In my mind, "pregnant" equaled "irresponsible." My friends were still able to enjoy life, have sex, and not live with the public humiliation because they were more "careful." And so I started forming a hardened view in favor of contraception. I could understand why everyone said to have "safe sex" because I was living the consequences of being irresponsible.

During my college years, I remember seeing a local doctor on television at a pro-life rally. He was talking passionately about the evils of contraception. For the life of me, I couldn't understand why he would speak against contraception at a pro-life event. I thought he was making a fool of himself. Though I was definitely against abortion, I couldn't see what was wrong with contraception. It seemed logical that if people used contraception responsibly, then there wouldn't be so many unwanted pregnancies and, thus, we would have fewer abortions. By this time I was working as an obstetrics nurse, and I saw so many babies born to single mothers. How my heart ached for these mothers and their children! I thought the answer was contraception.

In the midst of my confusion, sorrow, and brokenness, God

brought an amazing man into my life. From the beginning, though, we fell into sinful patterns and even moved in together. I rationalized our sexual activity because we were being "careful." At least I wasn't like the single women who came through labor and delivery, having child after child. I was proud that my first child was five and I had not had another baby. I was in graduate school working on my second master's degree, seeking to buy into the success the world had to offer. I was making something of myself, and that was all that mattered to me at the time. But I was not at peace.

I thought that marriage would bring me the peace I was searching for. Sex would be "allowed" and a pregnancy would be "acceptable." However, I had brought a lot of baggage about sex into our marriage. My life seemed empty, so I attempted to fill the void with a career. I saw myself as self-reliant; I was not interested in my husband "taking care" of me. I had hoped marriage would fill the deep void I felt. But when the void remained, I blamed my husband for not making me feel all the joys and bliss that I expected from being married.

Alone Again

I often dreamed of the family I had wanted as a little girl and of the family I had wanted for my son, Tyler. I blamed a lot of my unhappiness on the guilt I felt from my earlier pregnancy, and I thought the emptiness I felt would be filled with a new, "planned" baby. I dreamed about the perfect pregnancy, delivery, and homecoming. However, right before we found out we were pregnant, my husband needed to move five hours away for a four-month internship. With my husband out of state and me alone, pregnant, and working in an exciting professional environment, I bought even more into the world's views of success. I would find my happiness in this world. I wondered why I had imagined a pregnancy would be the solution.

My pregnancy was healthy, and my husband returned home before the baby was born. This delivery was going to be all that I missed with Tyler. Within forty minutes of arriving at the hospital, our son Logan was born. Holding him after he was born was one of the most precious experiences I'd ever had. I think some of what I had held back when Tyler was born poured out in that moment. I held the beauty of God. But in only a moment, my joy turned to sorrow and fear for our newborn's life, as pneumonia required that he be transferred to a hospital with more advanced neonatal care.

There were no flowers, no congratulations, and no happy homecoming. My husband left in the ambulance with our newborn son, and my mother brought me home. I remember walking by Logan's bedroom and aching to hold my baby. He was released on Good Friday and, although I was overjoyed to have our baby home, I mourned the loss of the homecoming I had dreamed of—one of the things I thought I needed to be happy.

Despite my graduate studies, I was still able to spend a lot of time at home. There was such a feeling of peace in being a full-time mom. It was the first time I really embraced motherhood. I even started to see it as a calling. But after all the years in college, attaining degrees that seemed important to my worth, not to mention the student loans, the possibility of ever being a stay-at-home mom was far-fetched.

A Light for Our Path

With the birth of our son and with Tyler at first communion age, we decided to start attending church. We went irregularly, which was fine with me. I feared getting too close to "holy" people. My youthful look would inevitably lead to questions about how old I was when I first became pregnant, and they would learn of my sins.

During this time, I met the pastor of a neighboring parish, and he asked me to describe my relationship with God. I was completely dumbfounded. This was the first time in my life that I realized that God was calling me to a relationship with Him. When a friend from grade school invited me on a retreat, I went with the hope of learning how to have a relationship with God. Confession was offered during the retreat, so I went. As soon as I sat down, I started crying hysterically. I knew that I needed to tell the priest about my premarital sex, and this time I needed to tell him that I'd gotten pregnant and had had a baby as a result. Before I started confessing, he took my hand and held it. I told him about the premarital sex, and the pregnancy, and my shame. He listened compassionately. He told me that when God created Adam and Eve, He saw them as being very good. He told me that what God saw in me was very good. In that moment, I experienced God's grace in a powerful way. All that I had searched for my entire life was to know that I was good and loved—not because I was "good" enough but simply because I was created in God's image.

During that confession, I came to terms with the sins of my past. I realized that everyone, even God, had already forgiven me. I was the only one still holding on to judgment. I didn't love myself, and I didn't know how God could, either. I also realized the shame and guilt that I had carried over from my first pregnancy had completely blocked my appreciation of God's love for me. My repentance allowed a ray of His light to penetrate deep into my darkened heart. Slowly, I started to believe some of the words He had written on my heart from before my birth. I was His, and He was protecting me.

As the wall of protection around my heart began to crumble, I saw my husband in a new light. I was slowly learning to accept his love, let my guard down, and be vulnerable. With two little boys at home, we decided to look into contraceptive methods. My doctor prescribed birth control pills. I filled the prescription, but kept the pills untouched on my dresser for almost a month. I kept rereading the pharmacy pamphlet, feeling uneasy about some of the possible side effects. I also thought about that doctor I had seen on television who spoke so forcefully against contraception. At about the same time, I saw a bulletin announcement about Natural Family Planning and decided to learn more about it. My husband and I hoped this would be a way to prevent more children by contracepting the "Church's way." We went to the first NFP class believing that two children were enough for us. During that first class, however, we began to see the attraction of being open to life and even having more children—later, of course. There was a truth in the class that we had never heard before, and we really wanted to try to trust God with our fertility.

Shortly after the class ended, though, our two-year-old was diagnosed as being on the autism spectrum. My despair was intense. I wanted more than anything to know that I would be able to have a relationship with my child. We again started to question if we should have more children. After much prayer and soul searching, I felt strongly that God did not want us to live in fear—and that He was still calling us to be open to life. I felt that if I held up my end of the bargain and "trusted" God, then He would hold up his end and give us a healthy child.

We were excited when I got pregnant and had our third son, Carter. The delivery and birth were wonderful! However, within the first few weeks of Carter's life, we knew he was not developing normally. He had some of the same social "red flags" as Logan, plus some additional problems with his muscles. I felt like the rug had been pulled out from underneath me. I cried for an entire weekend and many days after. Carter began physical, speech, and occupational therapy before he was even a year old. My full-time job was my sons' therapy. I felt abandoned by God; He was letting me down, just as my father had.

Backsliding

My husband and I had decided not to use NFP, but it wasn't long before we felt guilty about our decision. We knew there was truth in the teachings of NFP—and that we weren't following God's plan for our marriage. After much prayer and discussion, we began using NFP again. Within weeks, we discovered I was again pregnant. This was not our desire. (While NFP is typically ninety-nine percent effective, I was recovering from surgery at the time and was on several medications that affected my cycle.) Once again, we had been following the rules of NFP without understanding the "heart" of it. I felt as though I tried to trust God and follow His ways, but He left me stranded, overwhelmed, and now pregnant. Our youngest was only nine months old, with special needs, and I did not feel like a responsible parent. I started buying into my earlier concepts of pregnancy and contraception. I had a difficult pregnancy, and the therapy and doctor's visits for our other two sons seemed like too much at the time. Carter was only eighteen months old when our fourth son, Aidan, was born. We soon noticed that Aidan, too, had many of the same issues with muscle weakness, and he began therapy.

About this time, I read the book *Good News about Sex & Marriage* by Christopher West, which introduced me to the concepts of the Theology of the Body. I was inspired. So I began attending Theology of the Body classes at our parish and going to conferences. The Theology of the Body helped me to see my son as a gift, regardless of any developmental issues he may have. I was finally able to understand that Aidan's delays in no way reflected God's lack of love; I was able to let go of the anger. As the life-changing truths of the Theology of the Body started sinking in, my husband and I felt a strong desire once again to be obedient to God's will.

As I lived the madness of taking three children under the age of five to therapy sessions five days a week, the Theology of the Body was a saving grace for me. I was especially moved by Christopher West's CD *Woman: God's Masterpiece*, which presents John Paul II's profound insights on the "feminine genius." I wanted to be God's masterpiece! But I realized that I still had many wounds that needed healing. First among them: I needed to disown the childhood vow I had made never to trust anyone who could hurt me, including God. After much prayer, God showed me He had not abandoned me after all. I had focused all of my attention on the disappointments in my life, but God redirected my focus to the many miracles he worked.

The Blessing from My Fathers

As I write this, my father has been sober for more than fifteen years, and my relationship with him now is all that I had wanted as a child. On a recent occasion, he took my hand and told me how much he loved me and how much he cherished holding me as a baby. The deepest part of my heart clung to his every word. All these years, I've been longing to know that he loved me! As with my experience in confession with the compassionate priest, at this moment I experienced, through my own father's love, the love of God for me, His daughter.

Life as a single mother was tough, but God sent me an amazing husband who is on this spiritual journey with me. My marriage is much stronger than it ever would have been without the Theology of the Body. I now see my husband as the gift God has given me. Because of God's love and my new relationship with Him, I am now open and receptive to life and to the love of my husband. I am a totally different woman than the woman he married. We have a new respect for each other and our sexuality. Before we encountered the Theology of the Body, we saw NFP as just a set of rules to follow. Now, we appreciate NFP as a gift God has given to our marriage. How amazing it is that God allows us to play a role in creation! The days of feeling like pregnancy was irresponsible are so far behind me.

My oldest son, Tyler, whom I had at such an early age, has been an inspiration to me. Because of my experience with the Theology of the Body, I want to help him develop a healthy appreciation of God's gift of his sexuality. I feel called to participate in any ministry that will bring God's message of love for us and His plans for our bodies to my son and other children his age.

My son Logan, the child with whom I feared I would never have a relationship, turned out not to have autism after all. He and I now have a relationship that is deeper than I would think is humanly possible for a seven-year-old. He dreams of becoming a priest one day. Due to the amount of time that I spent in therapy with him, I never returned to work full time. My husband and I had to think of creative financial ways for me to be able to stay at home, but we have been blessed because we put our family's needs first and trusted God with our finances. God has been so faithful in this area.

Carter is doing amazingly well in preschool, and his neurologist believes that he will turn out fine. And Aidan, our three-year-old, no longer shows any developmental delays. Every little kiss or hug from him during the day is a reminder of God's love and the beauty of His plan for our lives. Though I once had other ideas about what would bring me happiness, I now couldn't imagine anything that would bring me as much joy as being at home with my children.

As I write this, I am about to give birth to our fifth child. This is the first pregnancy during which I have embraced the Theology of the Body with my whole heart. I believe that God has brought the Theology of the Body into my life to protect my marriage and my family and to give me a profound respect for the gift of life.

After four boys, we found out that we will be blessed with a girl. We have already picked out a name: Isabella Grace. (*Bella* means "beauty," and it is every little girl's desire to know they are beautiful and loved by God. *Grace* because my husband and I are now open and desire life only because of God's grace.) My desire is that her beauty will always be found in God and that she will always know and feel His love for her. As we await her birth, I feel for the first time in my life that I am becoming a daughter, God's daughter. I see now that the entire journey of my life has been preparing me to have a daughter. I had to know and appreciate His love so that I could pass it on to her.

The Theology of the Body has helped me realize the gift of life and the gift that my children are to me. I can't imagine our life without them, and I thank God for opening my heart to life. I know I am where God wants me; this is my calling. I am the mother that these four boys were supposed to have, and they are the children God desired for me! I no longer desire an exciting career because I know it would never compare to the completeness that I feel with them. Motherhood is my calling. God has shown his love for me a thousand times over through my children.

Understanding God's plan has given me the strength to be the woman God created me to be. It has helped me to tear down the protective walls that I had built around my heart. The Theology of the Body has helped me to stop grasping at love and to be the woman that God loved before the beginning of time. I now feel the words of His love written on my heart; I am loved because I was created in His image. I am seeing my worth with God's eyes. I have not lived unprotected; His protection was with me in my mother's womb. He saved my life then, and with much joy I proclaim that I am His!

Trust in the Lord with all of your heart, and do not rely on your own insight. In all your ways acknowledge him, and he will make straight your paths (Proverbs 3:5-6).

An Experience of Redemption

Sr. Mary Agnes Dombroski, DMML

Two of the most profound events of my life involved angels— one benevolent, one malevolent. I believe the actions of one resulted in a family member's being saved; the actions of the other resulted in an oppression in my own life that lasted for many years.

When I was a child, I recall hearing the story of some ambitious young boys who tested their skill and almost experienced tragedy. In the 1950s, this small group of boys used to go crabbing at their favorite spot, a ledge on the side of a building that rose some forty feet above the mouth of a river. Because of the height, they could cast out their lines far and snare larger crabs. When their bucket was full, they would take their catch to a local restaurant, and the owner would pay them for the crabs. What could be more attractive to teenage boys? They could have fun—and make money doing it.

Then one summer day, one of the boys lost his balance. He tried to regain his footing, but it was too late. He felt himself falling off the ledge. Suddenly, powerful hands gripped him by the shoulders and pulled him back, standing him upright on the edge of the bridge. When he looked behind him, he saw no one. He realized that his guardian angel had just saved him. That boy grew up to become my father, and I still thank his guardian angel for saving him that day. If that angel had not intervened, I would not exist.

Whether we know it or not, angels have a powerful influence in our lives. Sometimes they graciously intervene in a physical way, as they did with my dad. We like to hear angel-rescue stories such as this one. We need to remember, though, that some of the angels fell at the beginning of time and are our enemies—they seek to lead us away from God. In St. Luke's gospel, Jesus tells His disciples that He saw Satan fall from heaven like lightning (Luke 10:18). Also, St. John the Apostle writes in the book of Revelation that when Satan was thrown down from heaven, his angels were thrown down with him (12:9). These fallen angels—demons—are at war with the followers of Jesus (12:17). They seek to lure people into sin with their temptations, and they constantly try to distort the truth and lead people astray. Sometimes, in their efforts to entice Christ's followers to sin, they even attack them physically. My story involves such an attack. However, the real story is not what Satan did but what Jesus did to save me and make it possible for me to live the new life He had won for me on the cross.

Young and in Love

People who know me well tell me that my vocation story is romantic. It began when I was thirteen years old. I was sitting at my bureau one day, combing my hair and thinking about all of the wonderful marriages in my extended family. In a single moment, I was given an extraordinary understanding. At once, I saw how beautiful the sacrament of marriage is and how, through their love and faithfulness to one another, spouses love God, too. I also understood how marriage is the sign of the eternal love and communion we will share with God in heaven at the end of time.

I marriage is so beautiful, I thought, *and if I could love God through my husband, what about loving God directly, as I hope to love Him in heaven some day?* I always considered that moment to be Jesus' marriage proposal to me. I saw my vocation as a religious sister. Many years later, when I began learning about the Theology of the Body, I recognized many of Pope John Paul II's concepts in that moment of light I'd had as a teenager.

As I grew older and my hormones began to manifest themselves, I struggled with the idea of a religious vocation. Part of me wanted to get married and become a mother. By the time I graduated from high school, however, my mind was made up. Jesus was the only spouse who could satisfy my desires. While I waited for Him to show me the order he was calling me to enter, I promised Him I would marry no one else. As far as I was concerned, Jesus and I had eloped. Two years later, I entered the congregation Jesus had chosen for me.

In those teen years before I entered religious life, I struggled with the meaning of my sexuality and vocation, and I fell into sin for a brief time. Thankfully, confessions were heard before every Mass, and through the grace of the sacraments, I soon turned away from the sin into which I had fallen.

Many people do not realize how sin damages the soul. Though our sins are forgiven in the sacrament of reconciliation, some residual damage to our soul remains. That is why the priest assigns us a penance: to make satisfaction for our sins and help us "repair" our souls. Additional repair may be needed, though, for a person to overcome a particular vice and live a life of virtue. If a person builds a house with a small hole in its roof, then water will drip in when it rains. The residual effects of one's sins are like having a "hole" in the "roof" of our soul. For a long time, we may not even notice it is present. However, a vulnerability exists that may be exploited by the enemy.

This is how a demon entered into my story. I believe that if I had prayed more as a teenager, asking Jesus to repair the hole in my roof, He would have done so. Instead, a tiny seed of desire remained in my soul even after I confessed my sin and resolved never to commit it again. Because I was unwilling to let go of that tiny seed, I unwittingly prevented the hole in my roof from being repaired. I still had an attachment to sin.

Lust is part of our fallen, human condition. To be faithful to the teachings of Jesus in the Sermon on the Mount, we must overcome it. That means keeping a firm control over our desires and our will. However, sometimes the body is aroused sexually apart from—and contrary to—our will. Nonetheless, is it sufficient that the arousal was not wanted or desired, or are we obliged to bring our bodies to the point of integrity to which we aspire in our will? How can we achieve this bodily integrity when the physical sensations of lust often can seem beyond our control?

For a long time, I searched for answers to these questions, but my search was unsuccessful. I read many books defining sin and how to avoid it, and my confessors often gave me good advice about how to avoid near occasions of sin. The question of what to do when the body is physically aroused by lust, however, was never answered adequately. I also searched the lives of the saints. St. Francis of Assisi embraced a rosebush when he was aroused by lust, but that solution didn't seem practical to me. Other saints whipped themselves with cords, even to the point of drawing blood. Such corporal penance was forbidden by the rule of my religious congregation. Still other saints—St. Thérèse of Lisieux, for example—taught ways of becoming holy that were easy to understand and imitate, but none addressed my issue. I found myself tormented by my own vulnerability to failure, not knowing how to overcome it and unable to find answers anywhere I looked.

Then I began learning about the Theology of the Body, as taught by Pope John Paul II. I soon recognized that here was a man who had heard thousands of confessions and had wrestled with the same questions I had been asking. While the Theology of the Body answered my questions about how to overcome the physical manifestation of lust, it did much more. By sharing my story, I hope that anyone who has been wounded sexually or who is tempted heavily in sexual matters will be able to understand how real the salvation Jesus won for us is and how possible it is to live the resurrected to which God calls us in the Gospel.

Oppression and Redemption

My first real experience of the destructive power of lust happened when I was eighteen years old and part of a parish-outreach ministry. One of my assignments involved visiting an elderly man who lived in a home for the aged was homebound. On my first visit with him, he began discussing how he felt tortured by intense sexual desires and could find no relief. At that time, my parish had no training for the type of ministry I was doing, nor did I have a mentor with whom I could discuss the man's obsession. I should have brought the situation to my pastor's attention right away, but I did not know how serious the issue was. Instead, I listened compassionately to the man, attempting to change the subject each week. Eventually, he started to beg me to have sex with him every time I visited. The man was frail and in his nineties, so I had no fear for my safety.

Finally, the day arrived when I told him I was entering religious life and would no longer be able to come and visit with him. Much to my surprise, he suddenly went into a rage and began shouting curses at me. Startled, I quickly left. I thought nothing more about the incident. Now that I have worked in healing ministry, I know that curses can be real, but I did not know it then.

It is important not to dismiss the idea of a curse as something belonging to the realm of fairy tales. A curse is real and it involves two things. First, the person uttering the curse is wishing evil on the person to whom the curse is directed. In my situation, the old man was wishing evil upon me, particularly in relation to my religious life. Second, the uttering of a curse is an invitation for the powers of darkness (i.e., demons) to do what they can to make the curse happen. Satan and his army want to promote evil. If they hear someone wishing evil on another person in the form of a curse, they will be more than happy to jump right in and help the cause. In my situation, a demon had power *only* because I had retained an attachment to sin—the "hole in my roof"—that allowed what I believe was a demonic attack to take place, two years after I entered religious life.

One day, without warning, I felt as if an unseen perpetrator were raping my body. This sensation was not like an ordinary arousal that can happen sometimes. It was a far more aggressive experience than my own hormones could have brought about. I was extremely frightened. For a long time, I prayed to Jesus about this trauma, but it seemed to me that He remained silent.

As I began to learn more about healing ministry, I discovered that curses can have powerful effects and that demons can act through them. When Jesus healed me from this attack by driving away the demon, He also helped me understand that the man's curse had culminated in the attack. However, just as a battle can leave a soldier wounded, this assault by my invisible attacker left me wounded. I lost the beautiful vision of the body and human sexuality that God had given me at the age of thirteen. I now felt a rage against my own body; it had betrayed me. It would be many years before Jesus healed my wound through the Theology of the Body.

In my work and study of people who have been sexually abused, I have learned that many had similar feelings following their abuse. While they knew the abuse was wrong, they had strong sense of guilt because of the unwanted physical pleasure those moments of abuse had caused. As a result, they transferred the blame from their abuser to themselves. I discovered that abused people typically have feelings of rage against their own bodies because they feel their bodies have betrayed them. Many of them turned to sexually deviant behaviors so that they could feel more control over their sexual urgings.

The rage I felt against my body caused me to feel distant from my spouse, Jesus Christ. I wanted to live my vow of chastity, but I felt my Divine Bridegroom had let me down by not protecting me. I also felt that Our Lady had let me down. Prior to the assault, I had what I thought was a strong and loving devotion to her. Afterward, I could not understand how my beloved heavenly Mother, whom I had trusted so much, could have allowed this trauma to happen. I still did not understand that I was the one who had allowed the hole in my roof to stay there, because I had not totally renounced the desire I'd had when I sinned as a teenager. Although I was living in grace and remained close to the sacraments, especially the sacrament of reconciliation, I seemed to be alienated from my supernatural family.

Another result of the physical assault on my chastity was that I no longer believed strong temptations to lust could be overcome. Long after the demon was gone and forgotten, if I was awakened during the night by strong feelings of lust, I would try to ignore these feelings and get back to sleep without giving in to them. Inevitably, though, the belief that these lustful feelings were impossible to overcome would win, and I would give in to the sexual urge so that I could sleep. I was afraid of trying to stay awake and fight the lust, because it reminded me too much of the assault I had experienced. I felt defeated and paralyzed. I continued to plead with Jesus to finish the healing He had begun when He delivered me from the demon. I knew I could not stay in this place of compromise with lust.

Discovering a New Way

One day, a friend told me about a set of videotapes she had recently obtained on Pope John Paul II's Theology of the Body. The presentations were by a man named Christopher West. She highly recommended them for our sisters, saying she had cried joyfully through every talk. "Everyone should hear this message," she said. I had never heard of the Theology of the Body, but I returned home, spoke to my superior, and placed an order. The first time I watched the presentations, I was mesmerized, and I ended up watching them several times. I also began reading John Paul II's book, *Theology of the Body*. Although I found the Holy Father's writing difficult to understand, I began to comprehend his vision of the holiness of the human body, and I began slowly to heal. I remembered the grace of understanding I had received at age thirteen and realized that God was giving back to me the understanding I had lost.

I started to appreciate the humanity of Jesus in a way I never had before. The story of the fall of our first parents, described in the book of Genesis, came to life for me as I read and listened to John Paul's explanation. I believe it was the first time in all my Catholic upbringing that I understood the nature of original sin and how it affects our human nature. The fact that Jesus came into our fallen world and took on our human flesh suddenly had new meaning for me. The biggest surprise for me in Christopher West's presentations, however, was that Jesus had been crucified without a loincloth.

Like most Catholics, I understood the connection between the cross and the Garden of Eden. What I had never realized was that the first consequence of the sin of Adam and Eve was the distortion of their understanding of their sexuality. Before the Fall, they could look at each other's nakedness and see God's beautiful plan—namely, that they were created to love as He loves. After the Fall, though, when they beheld the other's nakedness, they experienced lust. That is why they immediately sewed fig leaves together: to protect themselves from the lust of the other. Lust reduces human dignity by turning a person into an object for someone else's gratification. On the cross, Jesus restored the original meaning of our sexuality and gave us the power, through grace, to live the meaning of our sexuality in the way God had intended it when He created us in His own image to love as He loves.

We will not experience the redemption of our sexuality in its fullness until we are in heaven. However, even now, we can begin to experience the power of redemption, won for us by Jesus on the cross, to overcome lust. This particular aspect of our redemption must have been extremely important to Jesus, since He chose to allow Himself to be crucified without a loincloth. Suddenly, I no longer felt distant from my spouse. In fact, He was so interested and concerned about my broken humanity and my struggle with the meaning of my sexuality that He was willing to expose His own nakedness to the whole world so that I could regain my dignity.

This realization healed the distance I had felt in my relationship with Jesus. I now knew that He intimately understood everything I had been through. I also knew that He had invested much more effort into helping me overcome lust than I had. The rage I felt against my own body began to melt away as I continued to contemplate Jesus crucified. I knew my body had been created for holiness, and I began to understand the price Jesus had paid so that I could become holy—not just in my spirit but in my body as well. Contemplating Jesus on the cross also brought healing to my relationship with Our Lady. I had loved her as a child and as a young adult, but when the assault on my chastity and the struggles I experienced after that came, Our Lady seemed too pure and remote for me. After all, she had never sinned. Her motherhood was supernatural, and she gave birth to Jesus without her virginity being compromised. How could she relate to me, when I was so deeply wounded in my sexuality? Why had she not protected me?

It was by standing at the foot of the cross next to Our Lady in prayer that I began to recognize my error. A great war was going on, and I had been involved in one battle. Jesus had already won the war by His victory on the cross. He went before all of His followers into the thickest part of the battle, and Our Lady was beside Him every step of the way. The wounds inflicted on Jesus' flesh were carved as deeply on Mary's heart. One demon had assaulted me, but Mary had watched a multitude of demons incite the soldiers to horrific cruelty as they scourged Jesus, crowned Him with thorns, and nailed Him to a cross. Mary no longer seemed remote to me. Instead, my sufferings seemed small compared to her sufferings at the foot of the cross.

Furthermore, Our Lady had accepted the task of mothering me when Jesus said to her, "Woman, behold, your son!" (John 19:26). I realized she had protected me from the loss of my vocation and from turning to a life of sin. Standing at the foot of the cross with Mary, I saw the hole in my roof and repented more deeply for my sins of the past. Without her help, I would not be giving this witness today.

Removing the Thorn in My Flesh

The Theology of the Body brought healing into my life from the first time I heard this profound message. I overcame the rage I felt against my own body, recovered the beautiful vision of sexuality I had understood as a child, and again enjoyed close relationships with Jesus and Mary. I also had a new appreciation for what had happened to me. A passage that St. Paul wrote about his own, similar trial resonated with me:

> A thorn was given me in the flesh, a messenger of Satan, to harass me, to keep me from being too elated. Three times I besought the Lord about this, that it should leave me; but he said to me, "My grace is sufficient for you, for my power is made perfect in weakness." I will all the more gladly boast of my weaknesses, that the power of Christ may rest upon me (2 Corinthians 12:7-9).

Before I learned about the Theology of the Body, "grace," as spoken of in this passage, was a remote and abstract concept to me. Pope John Paul II helped me understand the power of God's grace. Christopher West, through his eloquent explanations of the Holy Father's teachings, showed me how to apply the power of that grace to situations that troubled me.

The healings I received were significant. However, I was still living in a compromise with lust. The Theology of the Body had changed my life intellectually, spiritually, and emotionally, but I had not yet physically integrated what I had learned. I still did not believe lust could be overcome. Therefore, I continued to pray for healing in this area. One day, I viewed Christopher West's DVD presentation *Winning the Battle for Sexual Purity.* He was speaking to a group of men, and he suggested that they should stay in the shape of a cross for as long as it would take for Jesus to completely overcome the lust they were experiencing in a given moment. After watching this presentation, I understood that if I was to win the battle against lust, there could be no compromise. Besides suggesting that we stand in the shape of a cross, West reminded us that we had to believe in the power of Jesus to save us. We were not to empty the cross of its power (see I Corinthians 17). Finally, he taught that if our slavery to lust was based in fear—as mine was—then we had to face that fear. Here, at last, was the answer I had been seeking: a practical way to overcome lust the moment I experienced it in my body. I decided to follow his suggestions, no matter how difficult they were.

The next time I was awakened during the night with strong feelings of lust, I got up right away and laid down with my back against the hard floor in the shape of a cross. The hardness of the floor made me more aware of the cross of Jesus. Putting my body in the shape of a cross was a powerful reminder that I could not win this battle on my own; I had to allow Jesus to win the battle within me. In John 15:5, Jesus said, "Apart from me you can do nothing." I had finally reached the point where I knew Jesus' statement was absolutely true. Spiritually, at that moment, I was at a place I had never been before. I had no power on my own to win this battle. Once again, I contemplated Jesus' nakedness on the cross, and I realized that this struggle of mine was important to Him. His nakedness was proof to me that physical integrity is important, even if the body is inflamed with lust. The fact I did not want the lust was not enough; Jesus had given me so much more.

I prayed as I had never prayed before, really believing that Jesus had given me the grace to win victory over lust. I became determined not to give up until Jesus won that victory in me. I experienced the usual fear, but I was committed to facing that fear head-on, even if it killed me. I resolved to lie on the floor in the shape of a cross all night, if necessary. In fact, I stayed there only an hour. For the first time, the lust slowly receded and went away. I returned to my bed peacefully and fell asleep.

Since that night, I have tasted the victory that Jesus won for us on the cross. I am a witness that lust can be overcome. I have firmly resolved to never let my guard down and to engage in the battle whenever it comes. I no longer live in the defeat and paralysis that followed the trauma in my life. Believing that Jesus could redeem my sexuality helped me trust Him with other aspects of my life. This spiritual place, where I came to see that I cannot win the battle on my own but that Jesus ardently wants to win it for me, is a powerful place. I now go there every time I face a struggle that is hard to overcome.

The Theology of the Body transformed my life. I was broken and wounded, living in compromise with lust and feeling alienated from Jesus and Mary. Through the teachings of Pope John Paul II, so eloquently and passionately taught by Christopher West, I overcame the rage I had felt against my own body and recovered a sense of reverence for God's gift of my sexuality. I understood how God has called us from the beginning to love as He loves, and how, through His death on the cross, Jesus gave us the power to live our sexuality as God had intended from the beginning. Through the Theology of the Body, I saw the humanity of Jesus in a new light and realized how intimately Jesus and Mary understand our sufferings and our struggles. Finally, the Theology of the Body taught me to trust Jesus with a radical trust and to engage in the battle for sexual purity with a firm faith and a willingness to risk everything and to face my deepest fears, so that I may gain the victory Jesus has won for me.

The Theology of the Body and the Whole of My Life

The Theology of the Body did not just help me with sexual issues, however. Through it I learned to integrate other parts of my life with a much deeper faith. I learned the importance of taking care of my body to preserve my health. I also learned how to face a devastating illness, and to live with the chronic limitations that this illness caused.

A few years before I was introduced to the Theology of the Body I became a runner to help the children I was caring for at St. Charles Children's Home. We were working with some children who were pretty aggressive, capable of injuring not only other children, but also the staff. Almost every day we had to physically restrain one child or another who was out of control. The sisters sat down with the children one day in a family meeting, and did a brainstorm to figure out some ways we could decrease violence in our family. Many ideas were generated; they all had to do with finding ways for angry kids to expend energy in non-violent ways, such as riding a bike, bouncing a basketball or jumping rope. A day or so after our family meeting, I left for two months to return to our motherhouse to prepare for final vows.

Little did I know, life at St. Charles would not be the same when I returned. During that summer, the sisters began implementing some of the ideas generated at that family meeting. The only problem was, when kids are really angry they don't *want* to bounce a basketball or ride a bike: they want to pound someone's face in! To try to re-channel their energy and keep them from hurting the other children, Sister Maximilian began taking two of the most aggressive girls on a long walk in the woods every afternoon. By the end of the summer, those daily walks had turned into slow runs. When I returned to St. Charles after taking my vows, all of the children were running three to four miles a day with the sisters!

Now, I was not the athletic type. In high school, I avoided sports like the plague. I admired the kids who ran on the track team, but I never aspired to be one of them. In fact, I did not even believe I was capable of running. What a situation I was faced with when I returned home at the end of that summer! All of the children were good at running by then. Not only that, but the sisters who ran with the kids now had a kind of natural authority with them—a result of pounding the pavement together every day. If I did not take up running, the kids would know that they were stronger and faster than I was, and I would miss out on that prime time the other sisters were spending with them each day. Besides, I couldn't let Sister Maximilian be faster than I was. I took up running the day I came home.

My first run was three miles. In fact, I ran three miles every day for the next thirty days. I also hobbled around with sore muscles and took Tylenol every day that first month. After that, the run became one of the high points of my day. I even *almost* beat Sister Maximilian in one road race, but she passed me about twenty yards before the finish line.

My happiest time was the summer of 1999, when I discovered the Theology of the Body. My pleasure in running took on a whole new dimension. As I grew in reverence for the meaning of my body, athletic activities became acts of praise. I was running eight miles a day, four in the morning and four in the afternoon. Every afternoon that summer I also hiked for about two hours with some of the children who were afraid of the swimming pool. We had two favorite spots: one was a mountain that was absolutely covered with blueberries. We would climb the mountain, eat our fill of blueberries, and then return home in time for supper. Another favorite spot was by a river. There was very little rain that summer, and the river bed was almost dried up. We would walk on stepping stones for about a mile right down the center of the river. It was our daily adventure.

In 2001, the Theology of the Body helped me to make one major decision regarding my health. Though I was a runner, I still had a distorted view of the body and its role in my life. I had the idea that the body should be used until it wears out . . . that was my idea of holiness. I assumed that spending myself in ministry to the maximum degree possible was what God wanted. Like most Americans in our overactive culture, I did anything I could to keep my body going at the speed I wanted it to go. To put it simply, I was addicted to chocolate and caffeine. Unfortunately, I also had severe hypoglycemia, which was causing me to have blackouts almost every day. Eventually, I had to stop driving, since the possibility of a blackout would put my passengers in danger.

Then I learned of a naturopath doctor who could treat hypoglycemia. The treatment would involve my following a very strict diet. Without the understanding I had gained from Theology of the Body, I would not have gone to this doctor. Instead, I would have assumed it was God's will for me to be sick. But now I understood that my body was an important part of who I was, that it was a gift given to me by God. No one likes to give a gift to someone and then watch that person destroy the gift. Yet here I was destroying my body with chocolate and caffeine, when I had a disease that I knew was becoming worse because of the way I was eating. I went to the doctor and began a program to cure hypoglycemia. It wasn't just about getting better. For me, it was about treating God's creation (my body) with reverence. That treatment was successful. I did not have to give up driving after all, and I rarely have blackouts now.

By 2002, I was reveling in my rapidly improving health as well as running. Things could not have been better. Between the strict diet I was following and the daily runs, I felt like all of my physical activities of each day were ordered toward glorifying God. I appreciated the freedom I was now living on so many levels. I felt like an eagle soaring in the sky. I had learned that making healthy choices could glorify God. Now I was going to learn to glorify Him through illness.

One morning, I got up to run but got no further than the front yard before I felt like my heart was being squeezed out of my chest. I walked very slowly back into the house. Later in the day when I was climbing a flight of stairs I couldn't do it, and had to sit down. This began a long series of trips to the hospital and to doctors. The eagle that had once soared in the sky had come crashing to the ground.

For about two years, I was extremely weak and would spend a good part of each day in bed. I was heartbroken when I had to stop working with the children, and all of the happy memories of running and hiking seemed very far away. Yet, during this period of suffering, I came to understand two important truths at a deeper level than I ever had before. The first was that I can do nothing without God. Easy to say, but I had been living my life as if I were the one accomplishing things, and God was just helping me here and there. Now I realized that I could do nothing apart from God. The second lesson I learned was how real God's love for me is. I used to think that I had to pray and work to earn God's love, but my illness helped me to know that God's love for me is unconditional. He loves me totally, even in my weakness and physical frailty.

In light of the progress I had made in learning to have reverence for my body and to make healthy choices, this illness seemed anticlimactic. In a sense, my body was letting me down again. I had put all kinds of effort into being healthy, and here I was: sick. As at other times in my life, I could only make sense of the suffering at the foot of the cross. Jesus had given His body up for me. Now He was asking me, in a sense, to give up the health of my body for Him, and to unite my suffering to His for the sake of the salvation of souls.

During these years of severe illness, the witness of Pope John Paul II was incredibly helpful to me. As his body declined, he never gave up, never stopped; he was not ashamed of his infirmities. The biggest struggle in my illness was riding the elevator chair in our house. How humiliated I felt at first to ride that chair! But in meditating on the cross and learning from the example of John Paul II, I began to see how this infirmity was also a valuable part of my journey.

I have recovered from much of that illness, but not completely. Now I find that every day I have to wrestle with the fact that I might not ever run again, and the hikes I used to do with the kids are a happy but distant memory. I am no longer a soaring eagle. Instead I am a little bird with a broken wing that spends all its time on the ground. However, the lessons I learned from the Theology of the Body remain as true for me now as they ever were: my body is a gift from God, and I treat that gift with reverence and respect. Following the directions of the doctor has a deeper spiritual meaning than it did before. Before the illness, when I did what the doctor said I enjoyed the positive results right away. Now, living with a chronic condition, I rarely enjoy real positive changes in my health. How much more, then, am I taking care of this body for the Lord's sake, and not for my own!

In my spiritual life over the past forty years, I have encountered few works that transformed my life. The Theology of the Body is one of them. It affected me spiritually, but, more importantly, it taught— and continues to teach—me how to incorporate spiritual truths into the parts of life that our culture tends to keep separate from God. Not only did the Theology of the Body heal my sexual wounds and help me learn to overcome lust, but it also helped me to rejoice in the gift of my body and to recognize the importance of doing what I can to preserve my health out of reverence for God, who gave me the gift of life and the gift of my body. Finally, when I was faced with an illness I could neither prevent nor cure, the Theology of the Body helped me remain at the foot of the cross and see the great value of suffering that is united to Jesus' passion and cross. With all of my heart I thank Pope John Paul II for the great legacy he has left to me.

A Scholar's Renewal

Michael Waldstein

As I sat in my favorite chair, enjoying a splendid view of the snow-capped Austrian Alps and reading to my wife, Susie, the words of Pope John Paul II, we knew that we were hearing something different from what we had ever heard before—different, yet profoundly rooted in Catholic Tradition. As both of us held advanced degrees in theology, we had studied many of the major schools of theological and philosophical thought. These words from John Paul II, though, impacted us in a way we never expected.

We had been married for eighteen years, yet a fresh wind suddenly blew into our marriage, a wind of spring, bringing with it an increase of life. We had two more children after we began our study of John Paul II's teaching, bringing the total to eight. The "revolution" of the Theology of the Body had reached into our rural Austrian home and fueled a journey that changed much of the direction of my personal and professional life. John Paul II's acute attention to the experience of man and woman, which we could verify or falsify in our own experience, and his profound sense for the beauty of love between man and woman affected us particularly. I distinctly remember my eyes being opened with regard to my wife, opened to what we were experiencing and opened to the beauty of our relationship.

I had begun studying the Theology of the Body after being

appointed as founding president of the International Theological Institute for Studies on Marriage and the Family in Gaming, Austria. John Paul II had asked the Austrian bishops to set up this institute, similar to the John Paul II Institute in Washington, DC. Its purpose would be to train a new generation of theologians who would apply the Church's teaching to modern questions related to marriage and the family. The International Theological Institute began its work in 1996 under the direction of Christoph Cardinal Schönborn, the archbishop of Vienna. I was told by colleagues at the John Paul II Institute that the Theology of the Body would be the most important magisterial text defining our mission. I followed their advice and studied it with great intensity. To say that I was dumbfounded by the depth and power of the arguments in this voluminous work would be an understatement.

As I continued studying the Theology of the Body, I realized that my entire academic career up to that point—the advanced degrees, the grounding in philosophy, the teaching at university, the position papers—were simply a grand preparation for the work I would be called to do with this revolutionary work of John Paul II. It was almost as if I had chosen courses and paths specifically to prepare me to focus my mind on this work. I now realize it was divine providence that had chosen the paths for me.

The Yellow Brick Road

In my last year in high school in Salzburg, Austria, I became friends with a seminarian who was an enthusiastic reader of the Swiss Catholic theologian Hans Urs von Balthasar. He showed me Balthasar's works, and my friend's infectious enthusiasm took hold of me. I was particularly struck by the clarion call sounded at the beginning of the first volume of Balthasar's theological aesthetics, *The Glory of the Lord*, in which he encourages theologians to overcome the narrow limits in which the dominant historical-critical study of Scripture has been imprisoned. These limits, Balthasar argues, were imposed by modern natural science with its mechanistic view of nature. In this mechanistic view, the body has no power to express the spiritual. Worst of all, in this view, it becomes impossible to understand the foundation of theology and, in particular, the idea that "the Word became flesh and we have seen His glory." Once natural science is finished with the flesh, flesh cannot reveal much at all, let alone the glory of God.

Balthasar proposed a study of Scripture linked with a richer understanding of nature, which he found above all in the works of German writer Johann Wolfgang von Goethe. The appearance of God's glory in the flesh is closely related, Balthasar argues, with beauty. Seeing this glory with the eyes of faith is analogous to seeing the beauty of nature and works of art. These ideas were not so clear in my mind then, but the desire to study Scripture awoke in me.

Before beginning Scripture studies in Austria, I wanted to spend a year abroad. I chose to attend the newly established Thomas Aquinas College in California. I liked it so much that I stayed there for all four years. This college seeks to give its students a broad and deep formation in the Catholic tradition. Its curriculum pays particular attention to the origin of modern natural science. I came to see that modern science had abandoned the rich account of nature given by Aristotle and developed in the Middle Ages by St. Albert the Great and St. Thomas Aquinas, among others. This abandonment happened not because modern science had proved Aristotle wrong, but because it had decided to pursue a particular end, namely, man's power over nature. Given this end, it was natural that the founders of modern science turned to mathematical and mechanical accounts of nature. If you want power, you will find the science that is suited to providing power, namely, mechanics. In an attempt to wrestle with this reductive view of nature, I wrote my senior essay on Balthasar's account of the revelation of God's glory in the flesh.

From Thomas Aquinas College, I went on to earn a Ph.D. in philosophy at the University of Dallas with a group of philosophers who belong to the realist school of phenomenology, a philosophy based on human experience and with which Pope John Paul II is closely associated. I did not acquire a comprehensive view of John Paul's thought then, but I did take a seminar that devoted a whole semester to studying his pre-eminent philosophical work, *The Acting Person*. I took a similar seminar on the philosopher Max Scheler's *Formalism in Ethics*, which is the subject of Karol Wojtyła's habilitation thesis, a second thesis written at European universities after the doctoral thesis to enable scholars to assume a professorship.

We studied many other texts of the phenomenological tradition. The topic of my doctoral thesis was Balthasar's philosophical aesthetics, particularly his account of beauty in terms of expression and form (*Gestalt*), which is based on Goethe's understanding of nature. Goethe's understanding converges in many ways with that of Aristotle and St. Thomas.

Synthesizing my Thomas Aquinas College and University of Dallas backgrounds meant wrestling with the relationship between Thomism and phenomenology. This relationship is a key issue in reading the Theology of the Body.

I continued my studies, earning a licentiate in Scripture at the Pontifical Biblical Institute in Rome and a doctorate in New Testament at Harvard Divinity School, becoming more aware of the vast implications of Balthasar's clarion call for a reading of Scripture based on a richer understanding of nature.

When I began studying the Theology of the Body seriously in 1996, John Paul II's teaching had a tremendous impact on me. Here was a careful and full study of Jesus' teaching about the body, the main purpose of which was to show that "the body expresses the person," that it expresses and realizes the person's gift of self. The Word became flesh, and one *can* indeed see His glory in the flesh. In reading Genesis, John Paul II is able to show the powerful and deep beauty of God's plan for human love. He shows in actual practice what Balthasar's clarion call demands: passing beyond the mechanistic way of viewing the cosmos (and thus of reading Scripture) to a fuller grasp that is open to the beauty of creation.

A Gift to My Teaching, a Gift to My Life

I have taught the Theology of the Body consistently in my courses since 1996, often at the same time I am teaching a course on the gospel of John. At first, the Theology of the Body confounded me. It was hard work making my way through it along with my students. Soon, however, I was gripped by John Paul's penetrating account of experience and his sense for the beauty of love. The students were gripped, too. One of them told me she noticed that I now looked differently at my wife, that an intensity of relation was expressed in our glances that she had not previously seen.

During this time, a myriad of ideas about the convergence between

John's gospel and the Theology of the Body came to me. At a certain point, I knew I had to organize them in a single book. In doing so, though, I would run into some problems in my attempt to make progress with the Theology of the Body. I would later find out that others had experienced similar challenges.

Everyone who has struggled to read the Theology of the Body has had a similar experience at the beginning: It is like being far out in the ocean, in a fog, and with no compass to navigate. One does not know where one has come from and where one is going. I began to look for pointers in the text itself about how John Paul II structures his argument. The order of an argument is the key to understanding it. I drew up chapter and section headings in the English translation I was using to organize the pointers, but I was never fully satisfied with the results.

In addition, I became increasingly aware of problems in the existing English translation. As a result, I began to retranslate particularly important sections from the Italian text into English. I also began using these alternate translations in my classes, revising them as I restudied the text for a new semester. In the summer of 2004, I decided to contact the Daughters of St. Paul about these translation problems, as they were the publishers of the English text that most of the world had been using at this point. The Daughters answered that they had been praying about commissioning a new translation of the Theology of the Body and that my contacting them was providential. By the fall of 2004, I had formally started the project of the new translation.

From that point on, the Theology of the Body became my main occupation. I worked for two years on the translation. When I was translating the chapter about the resurrection, John Paul II fell into his final illness and died. It was an intense spiritual retreat to be completely immersed in his teaching about the risen body and its fulfillment in the Beatific Vision exactly at the time that the author of the work was—this seems certain—experiencing the Beatific Vision himself.

When I heard that John Paul II's secretary, Archbishop (now Cardinal) Stanislaw Dziwisz, had decided not to burn John Paul II's papers, contrary to John Paul II's wishes (Cardinal Dziwisz said afterwards he found nothing worthy of burning), I thought that perhaps somewhere in these papers I would be able to find an outline of the original work. It seemed likely the pope would have had an outline when he wrote it. After many mishaps and unsuccessful attempts, I found the original Polish typescript of the Theology of the Body in the archives and learned that it had been written before John Paul II was elected.

This discovery was contrary to what the Vatican's Secretariat of State and even the director of the archives had told me: the original language of the Theology of the Body, they had said, was Italian. On the basis of this conviction, the head of the Vatican archives assumed that the Polish version was a translation from the Italian. I now understand what the Secretariat of State meant when he told me that the Italian text was the original: the Italian version is the text officially pronounced and promulgated by John Paul II; it is the original text in the sense of being the authentic and authoritative text. The discovery that the Polish text was original in a different sense—namely, in the sense of having been written earlier—showed me the importance of the following discovery.

The Polish typescript has an elaborate division of the whole into two parts, each of them three chapters, with many sections and subsections, five levels deep. I had found the key I was looking for. Both the Italian and the English editions had divided the work into six "cycles," but these differed in important ways from John Paul II's own division. For example, the section on celibacy for the kingdom is a subsection in John Paul II's chapter on the resurrection, but a separate cycle in these earlier editions. In addition, these editions lacked the division of the whole work into two parts and the five level subdivisions of each chapter. I also found that this key had been available all along in the Polish edition of the Theology of the Body, published by the Vatican in 1986. The Polish edition's headings had never crossed the language barrier into any other edition, not even the edition of the Italian text, because everyone wrongly assumed that the Italian text had been translated into Polish and that these headings had been added at that time. The opposite is true: the original Polish headings had been omitted when the text was translated into Italian. This discovery was immensely exciting, because so much that had seemed obscure became clear. I was no longer adrift in a vast ocean. Not only had the fog subsided, but my radio had come back on stronger than ever and I could see a lighthouse in the distance.

I can now see that the Theology of the Body is a carefully constructed and rigorously written work. Emory University's Luke Timothy Johnson, a New Testament scholar, who has provided many sensitive and penetrating commentaries on books of Scripture, wrote a review in *Commonweal* in which he calls the Theology of the Body "mind-numbingly repetitive." Many others have had a similar impression and, partly for this reason, the Theology of the Body has received little attention from academic theologians, with the exception of some who are associated with the John Paul II Institute. It is clear to me now that John Paul II's masterwork is one of the rare seminal and epoch-making works of theology that richly repay careful academic study. George Weigel's striking image of the Theology of the Body as a ticking timebomb aptly describes its impact on academic theology.

Dr. Michael Waldstein is a distinguished fellow of The St. Paul Center for Biblical Theology and St. Francis of Assisi professor of New Testament at the International Theological Institute in Gaming, Austria. He holds a BA from Thomas Aquinas College, a doctoral degree in philosophy (PhD) from the University of Dallas, a Licentiate in Sacred Scripture (SSL) from the Pontifical Biblical Institute in Rome, and a doctoral degree in New Testament and Christian Origins (ThD) from Harvard University. He and his wife, Susan, are members of the Pontifical Council for the Family and have eight children.

An Unexpected Love Affair

Vicki Larson

As a Christian, I firmly believe that God is a God of love—but He can act in ways that, at first, seem anything but loving. For most of my life I was a comfortable Christian. I had a great husband, captivating kids, and a good spiritual life, but God was calling me to something more—something I could have never dreamed of. And he did it through a most unusual and unexpected way.

I was a lifelong Lutheran until March of 2005, when I stood in front of a Catholic pastor and professed to accept and live all that the Catholic Church taught and believed. If you had asked me a few years earlier if I would ever become Catholic, I would have laughed out loud. In fact, I clearly remember when, after a four-year struggle that began around 2001, I lamented to a friend, "Please pray for me to know the church that God wants us to belong to." She responded with what I thought was a preposterous statement: "You should consider the Catholic Church." At that time, Catholics were somewhat of a joke to me. I saw most as being Christian in name but barely so in practice.

I attended a Lutheran high school in a rural part of South Dakota. My future husband Bruce (also a lifelong Lutheran), and I met while attending a Lutheran liberal arts college in Minnesota. We married in 1972 and soon moved to Fargo, North Dakota, where Bruce had been offered a coaching and teaching position at a Catholic high school. (As one of the few non-Catholic faculty members, Bruce was exposed to Catholic practices I found odd and even sacrilegious. In hindsight, God was undoubtedly planting seeds in Bruce's heart, seeds that would bear fruit many years later in his openness to the Catholic faith.) Over the next twelve years, we were blessed with three beautiful children. In 1984, I began a fifteen-year career as a parish educator in the Evangelical Lutheran Church of America (ELCA).

The ELCA is one of several offshoots of Lutheranism. While labels are often misleading, one could accurately describe the ELCA as one of the more "liberal" Lutheran churches—especially in comparison with the other major national Lutheran body, the Lutheran Church Missouri Synod. As is the case with every Lutheran group, we believed our particular branch was the proper way. In time, I would seriously question this belief, due in no small part to the denomination's weakening position on pro-life issues, in which I believed strongly.

Life was good for our family. Our three daughters—Karin, Anne, and Sara—were thriving. My work was rewarding, and in 1987, my personal faith reached new heights after attending a Billy Graham Crusade, during which Bruce and I made a profound recommitment to Christ. After this renewal, I had an insatiable desire to read Scripture. In time, I could speak with authority on certain theological subjects.

For nearly seventeen years, beginning in 1980, I was heavily involved both as a member and later a leader in a large, highly organized non-denominational Bible study called Bible Study Fellowship (BSF). During those years, I invited many people to join, including some of my Catholic friends. My knowledge and love of Scripture and the Lord continued to increase. Bruce eventually joined BSF, and I saw the Holy Spirit begin to work in him as well.

The Search for a New Spiritual Home

Around 2000, after a closer look at the ELCA's stand on life issues, including abortion and homosexuality, Bruce and I began to discuss seriously our dissatisfaction with our denomination's official positions. It is one thing for individual members of a congregation to be confused about moral questions; it is quite another for one's denomination to officially embrace overt moral evils as policy. We understood the principle of the "slippery slope" and wondered what positions our church would adopt next. Our dilemma was that if we remained members of the ELCA, we were giving at least tacit approval to the denomination's erroneous positions, and our consciences would never be at peace. Yet we didn't know where to begin to find "the right church," one that taught Christian orthodoxy but that also appealed to our human needs.

For more than four years we prayed for God to direct us to the right church. During this time, we started attending an Evangelical Free Church (EFC). I vividly recall putting a prayer card along with our tithe in the offering plate, asking for the Lord's guidance. Despite some good fellowship, this particular church did not reach our hearts and minds, so we eventually left. The years following our departure from the EFC were lonely, as if we were in a desert. Each Sunday morning we would face the question, where shall we worship today? Even though most of the churches we attended were clearly Christ-centered and populated with godly people, something substantial was missing.

In 2000, we also began to spend many weekends out of town. Our youngest daughter, Sara, had started college that fall at Augustana College in Sioux Falls, South Dakota, and had become a member of the volleyball team. Wanting to support her, we took a host of short trips to the towns where she played. One benefit of being away was that we could attend a variety of churches. We went to Lutheran, Baptist, Evangelical, and non-denominational churches, reading doctrinal statements to see if we agreed with them. We found anything but that unity for which Jesus had prayed to His Father in John 17.

Finally, we came to understand that we should be under the authority of a *church*, not a particular pastor. Today, as a Catholic, I clearly see that this realization was a movement of the Spirit in our lives. We concluded, if we join a church because we like the pastor's beliefs, homilies, etc., what would happen if that particular pastor left? Would we still follow the teaching of the particular denomination?

We then began to reflect on why good, sincere Christians—all of whom were saying Scripture was their only authority—could so radically disagree on important doctrines, such as whether a Christian could lose his salvation and whether the Eucharist was just a symbol or truly the body and blood of Jesus. Surely, we decided, Jesus had to offer a better way of knowing what was and was not true. We also realized that just because we believed something was true did not, in fact, make it true. There had to be a more objective standard. With each passing month, we were getting hungrier to know the truth. But which church possessed it? We couldn't imagine that Jesus did not leave us a sure path to follow.

A Theology with Life-Changing Answers

Amidst the uncertainty of the search for a church, God opened up an opportunity that changed my life. Although I had always believed in the chastity message—that sexual virtue was important, especially before marriage—I was led down a path that many experience once they embrace this message more fully: the scales began to fall off my eyes and I saw the dramatic ripple effects of sexual sin in our culture and in my own life.

In 2001, I was hired as the director of the "abstinence until marriage" outreach at a local Christian pregnancy clinic. I learned so much about sexuality, marriage, and virtue in my first year there. Frankly, my appetite for truth in these areas was insatiable. I read books and pamphlets, listened to audiotapes and CDs, and watched DVDs at work and at home. Each time my husband and I got in the car to travel to one of our daughter's volleyball games, I stocked up on CDs and tapes for the trip. The speakers were from varying faith backgrounds and approached the topics from so many wonderful perspectives. To my surprise and delight, Bruce enjoyed them as much as I did.

Together, we learned much about the theology of marriage. We reveled in reflections on how earthly marriage was a reflection of the inner life of the Trinity itself. We came to see that the one-flesh union was sacred and holy and that it, too, was a dim foreshadowing of the Trinity. I began to use terminology that was a bit foreign to the evangelical world, words like "marriage is a sacrament."

The pregnancy clinic's director was a Catholic. One day, she handed me a small case of audiotapes entitled *Pandora's Pillbox*. Produced by the GIFT Foundation, the tapes included a number of speakers, including an enthusiastic young speaker named Christopher West. The tapes were on a collection of works by Pope John Paul II known as the Theology of the Body. One particular talk by Christopher, "Marriage and the Eucharist," absolutely floored both Bruce and me.

He spoke of how our masculine and feminine natures were intended to be complementary. I had never heard anyone speak of sexuality from a Christian perspective as he did. We began to see the logic behind the traditional Christian teaching against contraception to which, apparently, only the Catholic Church continued to adhere. So many glorious things about marriage were revealed.

Bruce and I were fascinated at how the Bible both began and ended with a "marriage" and how this theme of God's wanting spiritually to espouse humanity ran through the whole of Scripture. We learned how Jesus' first miracle was at a wedding and how the multiplication of the wine at the wedding was symbolic of Christ's grace being offered to us in superabundance. Frankly, at this point, a small pit in my stomach began to form. Although I loved what I was hearing, I struggled that all this good theology was coming from a Catholic source. And I began to wrestle with my own contraceptive choices, past and present.

One day, as we traveled to my husband's family farm, we listened to Christopher explaining Edith Stein's hypothesis of original sin. A knife pierced my heart as I was convicted of my own sin. Later that same day, as we sat around the kitchen table, the conversation turned to our search for a church. Someone asked, "What church do you think you will end up in?" I responded, "I haven't said this, even to Bruce, but I think the Catholic Church." I shocked myself with these words.

During this time, we also painfully understood how we had denied God children that He may have wanted us to have. We had not trusted Him, sterilizing our sexual union throughout our marriage. It hurt. We got on our knees before the Lord to confess and tearfully repent. We also began to understand that contraception was really at the root of so many societal ills, from the proliferation of abortion, to divorce, to the growth of pornography, and more. Contraception turned sex from a paradigm of self-donation to self-gratification, often at the expense of the other.

The Theology of the Body was *all* I wanted to think about, talk about, read about, and listen to. In the fall of 2002, our eldest daughter, Karin, was moving to Colorado to teach elementary art. She had grown weary of my constant "chatter" about the Theology of the Body and finally said, "Just let me listen and decide for myself!" With a fourteen-hour drive ahead of her, I handed her the stack of tapes. After listening to the presentations, her immediate response was, "This makes so much sense!"

Karin was really starting to blossom spiritually, and our conversations revolved around what she learned in Bible study and how the Theology of the Body was evident in the writings of the Old Testament prophets. She, too, began struggling with the frustration of trying to find a church. There seemed to be such casualness and even a lack of reverence in many worship settings. She was praying for the same direction we were, asking, *Lord, where do you want me to go?*

That same fall, I attended a seminar by Christopher West in my home state of North Dakota. I was so excited to hear him in person. After his talk in Grand Forks, I was asked to drive him to Fargo, a seventy-mile trip. The poor guy had to listen to me rattle on for more than an hour about all that was happening inside of me. He patiently listened to me talk about what we had learned from the Theology of the Body. He said, "You have been bitten by the Theology of the Body 'bug.' Just keep saying yes to God, Vicki." I shared with him our conviction of the sin of contraception. He said he would pray for us.

Liturgy Leads Us Closer

We believe that, in the months that followed, God wanted to open Bruce and me up to the riches of the Eucharist. On one long road trip, we listened to a CD talk by Father Larry Richards unpacking the Mass. We began to see why one should genuflect when in the presence of the Eucharist and why only a priest or deacon should read the Gospel at Mass. We learned about the Real Presence and how this had been the belief of Christians since the time of the apostles. Everything had such deep meaning and significance. It was all so beautiful. I asked Bruce, "Does this make you want to receive the Eucharist?"

With no hesitation, he said yes. As Christopher had shared just a few months earlier—"Just keep saying yes"—I was hearing those very words from my husband's lips. Was our search for the truth leading us into the Catholic faith?

In January 2004, I attended a pro-life conference in Minneapolis. Archbishop Harry Flynn celebrated the Mass at the conference. During the liturgy I observed how he and the four other priests washed their hands with holy water shortly before and after the consecration. I saw them receive their Lord in the Eucharist before the congregation. I understood that this was the way God had instructed the Hebrew priests in the Old Testament to carry out their sacrificial sin offerings on behalf of the people. I was struck by the faith of the bishop, priests, and congregation. Frankly, it was markedly different from anything I had ever seen in my Lutheran church, in both reverence and in the order of who received the Eucharist first. Now that I had a Theology of the Body lens through which to look at life, I saw this as a tangible example of "taking" versus "receiving." A divine order of initiation and reception was present in the Catholic liturgy. As a result, we began a deeper journey for us into a more traditional liturgical experience.

The Theology of the Body and Its (Glorious) Ramifications

In mid-2004, I learned that the recently formed Theology of the Body Institute, located in suburban Philadelphia, was going to offer a week-long immersion course in John Paul II's Theology of the Body, taught by Christopher West. My daughter Karin and I made plans to attend. Karin had continued on her journey into this teaching thanks to a Catholic young adult group in Denver. Her comfort level with Catholicism also was growing. Among other things, she had joined an ultimate Frisbee league with her Catholic friends. Her team was called "Hail Mary."

Shortly before the trip, I found myself in a Catholic bookstore in Fargo when the local bishop, Samuel Aquila, came in.

Bishop Aquila, prior to his appointment as bishop of Fargo, had been Christopher's boss when he served in Denver. I told the bishop of my upcoming trip to the Theology of the Body seminar and he was very encouraging. The bookstore manager asked for his blessing on all in the store. I came away believing that my upcoming trip was being blessed in a special way.

This thought proved to be prophetic. On the flight to Philadelphia, a further confirmation came in the form of the passenger sitting next to me. Not only was he a Theology of the Body fan, but he also was familiar with Christopher's work. We parted ways with a promise to pray for each other.

Excited and nervous, Karin and I arrived at the rural Pennsylvania retreat house. We would be among just four Protestants in a group of more than eighty Catholics. That first night put us at ease as we heard a song featuring the refrain, "Be not afraid," which was a major theme of Pope John Paul II's pontificate. These words spoke to my eager but trembling soul, giving me a peace that would usher in one of the most extraordinary weeks of my life. I felt as if a perfect lover were wooing me. As in a courtship, I was scared but took each new step with anticipation. I wondered, *Is this the One I've been looking for? Is this the Church I am being called to?*

Each morning, we began the day with Mass. As we walked into the meeting room, I longed to dip my finger in the holy water but didn't have the nerve. What if one of the Catholics saw me and somehow objected? Karin and I observed the Mass and participated in ways that we could, such as kneeling and saying the Our Father. We observed the faithful as they received the Eucharist. Their bodies spoke a language that revealed their spirit. I was witnessing one of the sublime manifestations of the Theology of the Body in the very worship practices of the Catholics. The teaching throughout the week wove Catholic teaching in a tapestry that made so much sense.

In one of Christopher's first lectures, he explained a major difference between Catholic teachings and those of Martin Luther. Luther believed that humanity was totally depraved as a result of original sin. To show the utter depravity of humans after the Fall, Luther used the analogy of a heap of dung covered with a layer of snow, which was the grace of Christ. For the preceding fifteen hundred years, though, Christianity had a different view.

Prior to the Protestant revolution, all Christians believed that humanity—and the material world—remained essentially good even after original sin; they were, in the words of C.S. Lewis, "slightly bent."

In other words, the sin of our first parents left us with an inclination towards concupiscence—toward sin—but we remain fundamentally good. Baptism restores the sanctifying grace in our souls. Even though we will battle against the lure of sin in this life due to concupiscence, with God's grace we can substantially transform our "ethos," which is sort of like our internal operating system.

This concept—that we are good but "slightly bent"—was a revelation to me. Instead of being left with no hope of living a virtuous life, we can aspire to greatness, thanks to the grace of God. In my reflections during the Immersion Course, I realized that I had bought into the Lutheran belief of total depravity, as had my daughter Karin. I later learned that my baptism in the Lutheran church, since it was with water and the Trinitarian formula, brought about the same spiritual effects on my soul as Catholic baptism —even if I didn't know or believe this as a Lutheran.

On the third day of the course, a lovely lady invited me to pray during Eucharistic adoration. I told her I wasn't Catholic, and she said that didn't matter. I knelt alongside the dozens of Catholics present in the room, earnestly asking the Lord for healing for Karin and me.

When we went back to the room, we talked and laughed longer than we should have. The next morning, I woke up and went to breakfast, but Karin was completely wiped out. She hadn't slept all night. I told her to stay in bed, but I also thought that this could ruin the rest of the week for her. When I came back from breakfast, though, she was dressed, bright-eyed and ready to start the day. She said, "Do you know why I didn't sleep? All night long, I kept thinking, *I am good. You are good! We are good!*" Her words were a blessing from God and an answer to my prayers.

The teaching we learned that week was transformational, to say the least. We loved the idea that all humanity was called to a posture of receptivity, both in our relationship with God and with our fellow man. We learned that we are called to be fruitful, regardless of our vocation, and that we are "to love as God loves"—freely, totally, faithful, and fruitfully. What a beautiful message to hear.

During meals, we talked and listened. And we asked questions about the Catholic faith—tons of them. Never once were we made to feel like our questions were stupid. The love we felt from our fellow course attendees was the best evangelization we could have received.

Coming Home—To Fargo and to the Faith of the Early Christians

I returned to Fargo and Karin returned to Denver, with the same question: *Now what?* I realized that I was Catholic in my heart, but I knew Bruce was not there. Yet I wanted him to lead us on this journey. The unspoken tension between us started in earnest that first Sunday. Where should we attend church? As we backed out of the driveway, I was confused and discouraged. *Please, God,* I prayed, *show me if the Catholic Church is where you are drawing us. I need encouragement from YOU!* I did not say a word of this to Bruce. Nor did I know where he was driving us. Then I saw the sign for the Newman Center on the campus of Augustana College. We went in and sat in the back so we would not be noticed. We watched again in awe as people reverently received the Eucharist. I yearned to receive as well. Did they know that they had just taken the Lord of heaven and earth inside of them?

As we were leaving Mass, I encountered a young woman who was a former student of Bruce's and now a physician. I knew she had attended the same Lutheran college that we had. I asked her if she was converting to the Catholic faith and was surprised to learn that she had done so several years before, along with one of her brothers. She said her reading of the early Church fathers and Church history had led her to conclude that the Catholic faith was the one that traced itself back to the time of Christ and held to the beliefs for which those early Christians died. She was so excited to share her experience with us, and I left thanking God for this sign of encouragement.

That same night, Karin called from Denver to say that she had attended Mass at the Catholic cathedral that morning and that the homily was about the Assumption of Mary. The homily had summarized what we had learned at the Theology of the Body Immersion Course. As with the Assumption, the Theology of the Body is a glorious affirmation of the goodness and rich meaning of the human person, which can be seen in the Church's teaching that our bodies and souls will be reunited and "assumed" into heaven at the end of time. We saw our mutual attendance at Mass on this special feast day "of the body" as a sign that God was calling both of us into the Church. We felt as if we were coming home.

The pull toward the Catholic faith was so strong that I was consumed with reading as much as possible about the Church, exploring answers to our questions. I read books by Scott Hahn and Patrick Madrid's *Surprised by Truth*, among others. I came across a quote by famed apologist G.K. Chesterton that captured the essence of how we felt. "It is impossible to be just to the Catholic Church. The moment men cease to pull against it they feel a tug towards it. The moment they cease to shout it down they begin to listen to it with pleasure. The moment they try to be fair to it they begin to be fond of it. But when that affection has passed a certain point it begins to take on the tragic and menacing grandeur of a great love affair."[1]

Hoping that he could "bring us back to our senses," we thought it would be wise to tell a Lutheran pastor about what was stirring in us. We decided on a particular pastor who had a reputation for knowing and living his Lutheran faith. Since he did not know us well, we hoped this would make him brutally honest. He listened as I nervously explained what was happening. Suddenly, he got up and picked up a number of conservative Catholic books and publications off his desk to show us. He, too, was being drawn to the truth of the Catholic Church. What a wonderful shock and surprise! We were astounded at God's grace, and we left his office knowing we were on the right path.

Our journey moved from "dating" to "engagement." It was time to make a decision. The words "be not afraid" came to us. Our decision could separate us from our family and friends. We knew our conversion to Catholicism would be difficult for our parents, who over the years had heard so many negative things about the Catholic Church. But we knew it was our only option if we did not want to violate our consciences.

In the fall of 2004, my husband and I started RCIA classes in Fargo. Karin began taking similar instruction in Denver. In February 2005, the three of us made our first confession, followed the next morning by our first Mass. Receiving our Lord in this sacrament was all that we had expected it to be. We were confirmed in March, less than a month before the death of our new Holy Father, John Paul II. We felt blessed to have had him as our pope for even a few weeks. He

---

[1] *The Catholic Church and Conversion* (1929)

was the father of the Theology of the Body—the gift to humanity without which I may never have come into the Church. I will be forever grateful to the gift he has given me in this teaching—and the gift of the Church to which it led me.

The Long and Winding Road

Tanya Cangelosi

As I sat in the dark closet, I prayed to be freed from my captors and returned to my mother. Although I was told she was dead, I did not believe those whom I should have trusted. My captors were my grandparents. They should have offered me words of love, but they offered only harshness and abuse. As a little child, my prayers were not eloquent, but they were surely heard. In the years since my childhood, I have come to believe that our God is a gracious and loving God—one who seeks only our good, even if those to whom he entrusted my care abused the gift.

I am a witness to the power of the transformation that can come through a renewal of one's heart and mind. You see, if ever there were a "poster child" of a wounded soul who received healing through God's grace, it would be me. I was beyond lost. Today, despite the spiritual and emotional challenges I face, I am a woman who has tasted the good fruits God has to offer and desires nothing more than to pursue the love that truly satisfies the soul. Despite an unimaginable valley of death, I have experienced rich, lasting renewal, thanks in great part to Pope John Paul II's teachings known as the Theology of the Body.

I grew up in a suburban Chicago housing project named Manor Courts, where the poor whites lived. A few blocks away was Arsenal Courts, where the poor blacks lived. We kids of the projects did everything that our imagination could conjure up. Our behavior seemed "normal," though, because everyone around us was doing the same. The only "norm" we knew was what we saw on television. But even when I was quite young, my cynicism prevailed, telling me that television was just make-believe and that the images I saw were unreal. Even so, I pursued the lifestyle I saw on television as this was the only competing view to the madness I lived. But because I could never attain what I saw, I became depressed.

As an adolescent, I mimicked the language of the pimps who roamed the streets at night. Although the crowd seemed to like me, I always felt I had to prove myself to them. In short, I lived a depraved life, one filled with illicit sex, drugs, and alcohol. Today, I take great comfort in the teachings of Pope John Paul II, who said that even in these distorted pursuits, we are all actually searching for the "good." In our desire for "union and communion"—in our desire to "love and be loved"—we often settle for counterfeits. I have come to forgive myself and those who, in their distorted pursuits, abused me. I now know that the desires and hungers of the heart are not evil, even if they manifest themselves in evil ways.

My grandparents had fled from Bulgaria after my grandfather killed a man in a bar fight. They came to the United States, where they raised my father and my aunt. In Bulgaria, family loyalty is a great virtue, even if one of the family members is a bad egg. This loyalty would eventually cause my grandfather and grandmother to side with their son despite his physical and verbal abuse of my mom, my sister, and me.

My childhood and early teen years were horrific. Before my escapades as a pre-teen in the projects, my life was one filled with abuse. By the time I was three, the feuding between my parents had escalated to the point that my mother had finally had enough and divorced my father.

Since this was the mid-1950s, times were tough for a single, abused mother. She managed to get a job and secure a small hovel of an apartment for the three of us. But our situation improved only temporarily. My grandparents would babysit me from time to time, and they would often lock me in a closet as a punishment, although I am not sure how serious an offense a toddler could commit. If I made any noise in the closet, my grandmother would scratch on the outside of the door, pretending to be the *gritchen*, a Bulgarian bogeyman who terrified children. To this day, I am afraid of the dark and feel on edge in small rooms.

On one occasion, my grandparents put me in an orphanage, hoping that my mother would forget me and that they could legally adopt me. They told me that my mother had died and that my father, though he loved me, could not care for me. When I tried to tell the orphanage directors of my plight, they did not believe me, concluding that I was just a distraught young child.

Shortly after arriving at the orphanage, I stopped eating. After about six weeks of limited food, the orphanage directors put me in the hospital. I was suffering from malnutrition. The police soon came to know of my story and located my mother. I was returned to her and my sister, Maria. I was delighted to learn she was still alive! The years that followed were ones of constant fleeing from my father and grandparents. I specifically recall conversations between my mother and neighbors about my father's inquiries. We fled Illinois for Georgia, where a great uncle lived. He offered his assistance, and we jumped at the apparent gesture of kindness.

The time with my great uncle caused my life to spiral downward even more. During these years, when I was between the ages of three and six, this man committed the greatest of abominations: molesting me and allowing others to do the same. I suffered unspeakable violations in my own home and in his remote mountain house. The suspicions I had about men solidified beyond repair—or so I thought. By the time I was ten, I had tried to take my life several times. I also engaged in the now-common phenomenon of "cutting."

I was told never to speak of the abuse to my mother. Threats accompanied these demands. Seeking to protect my younger sister from the same abuse, I began to have a certain sense of power over the abusers, threatening them to stay away from her or I would reveal their crimes. I vividly recall one instance when my great uncle slapped my sister over and over, causing her to bleed from the mouth, because she would not eat a sandwich he had made. This time my threat of telling my mother about the abuse worked, and so I continued to keep quiet.

I came to believe at a young age, perhaps as young as six, that "sex" equaled "power." Although I may not have known those terms, the association was embedding itself in my already-warped psyche. By allowing the abuse to happen, I could control certain situations. I could stop a grown man from abusing a younger sister or secure an abundance of candy and even money from him. In these young years, I even began to understand survival skills, hiding the accumulated candy and cash and saving it for when I would need to buy loyalty or some other short-term solution.

This nightmare ended when my mother overheard me telling my uncle that if he didn't give me what I wanted (either more candy, money, or the like), I was going to tell my mother about the abuse. Late that night, she came to my room to ask me what the conversation with my uncle was about and if he had been touching me. I didn't know what to say, but I somehow managed to tell her the truth. That very night she chased him out of the house with a butcher knife—a traumatic sight for a six-year-old to witness. In my warped sense of love, I thought that this man who had abused me loved me.

The next day my mother took me to the hospital to be checked out. The doctor told her that I had been repeatedly raped, perhaps since the age of three. This was 1957. The doctor told my mother never to mention the abuse to me, indicating that talking about it would traumatize me more. I was thirty-four before my mother and I had a heart-to-heart on this issue.

To make matters worse, my uncle, before leaving the city, cleaned out the joint bank account he held with my mother. My mother was never good at paying the bills, but now we were so far behind there was no way out. Not only did we get kicked out of our house, but we also were escorted to the state line with a police car in front of our vehicle and one behind. I was embarrassed waving goodbye to all my friends as we pulled away from our house. We headed back to Illinois to return to the projects, moving into the downstairs apartment where we had lived before.

Here I met my father again, spending a week with him after I graduated from high school. The meeting was difficult and awkward. I didn't trust my father. He evidently didn't value me too much: I was assigned to sleep in a tiny room on a cot. I ended up calling my sister to come and get me. I simply couldn't stay in his roach- and mouse-infested hovel.

I learned through these experiences to be a survivor, to trust no one and to seek out friends I could boss around, use, manipulate, and terrorize in my desire to get what I wanted. I learned to steal, and I began to use sex to manipulate people and situations. I taught other children how to shoplift and would then take their stolen goods to the pawn shop. Many years later I met one of my thieving disciples. She had spent time in reform school because of her stealing habits. To this day, I pray for her and repent of having led her astray.

At twenty, I was unhappy, depressed, and extremely overweight. Weighing nearly three hundred pounds added to my mistrust of people, especially men. They couldn't seem to get past my body image to see the person inside. Though I had many male friends, none seemed interested in dating me. Desiring intimacy in any way that I could get it, I made myself available for sex. During tough financial times, I would request money in exchange for sex—even though I would have denied that this essentially made me a prostitute. During times of great emotional or financial desperation, I would go to a particular bar and offer my services. Too many times, I ended up in the back seat of a car or truck, a restroom, or an alley to make money but also to satisfy my need for love in a very warped way. I now see that I abused myself with this permissive sex as a means of revenge against my past, my family, and myself.

By my mid-twenties, I had ratcheted up my hard living. I rode a motorcycle, terrorized the timid, and hung out at bars where my friends and I drank and played pool. I was regularly using potent drugs and cheap liquor. Life was good, or so I thought. One stellar highlight was the time I drank so much whiskey that I passed out on a friend's porch for a full three days. My friends simply left me there, figuring that if I didn't wake up by the end of the third day they would call an ambulance. I had seen so many divorces, suicides, abortions, and acts of self-mutilation and overall depravity that I just wanted to leave this world. Thinking that whatever was out there had to be better than what I was experiencing, I ingested twelve bottles of various over-the-counter pills one night. I ended up in the hospital for nearly two weeks. If this was not the lowest point in my life, it was about as close to rock bottom as I could get.

Lacking the Look of Love

Many years later I heard of the story of Saint Nonnus of Edessa and Saint Pelagia. It is one that pierces the heart of any woman who has been used and abused. It also offers extraordinary hope for anyone who has been sexually wounded—or who has wounded another.

St. Nonnus was a fifth-century Catholic bishop who, through the grace of God, had come to understand deeply the plight of humanity. He saw that, despite the degradation all around him, God was the author of human life and that human life was therefore beautiful. He must have also had a particular insight into the pains of women. One day, Bishop Nonnus was walking with another cleric when both saw a beautiful woman—likely a prostitute—walking toward them. Not wanting to lust after this alluring woman, the companion of Bishop Nonnus turned his eyes away as she passed. After she had gone by, the companion saw that Bishop Nonnus had tears in his eyes. He also realized that the bishop had not turned his gaze away from the woman as she went by but had looked right at her. A bit baffled and concerned, he asked, "Brother bishop, why did you not turn away from this woman?" Nonnus replied, "What a tragedy it is that such beauty would be sold to the lusts of men." His response surprised the priest and, eventually, the woman herself.

This woman sought out Nonnus and, prompted by the loving response of the saintly bishop, experienced a conversion to Christianity. Despite her life choices, she experienced a piercing love in Nonnus' simple, chaste look into both her eyes and soul. We now know her as Saint Pelagia.

At that point in my life—and for the next twenty-five years—I do not recall having experienced this kind of look until I met Father Michael O'Loughlin, a man who would become my father in faith. He was the pastor of the parish where I would eventually make my home. If you had told me even a few years before that a man could look on me with love (as Father O'Loughlin does with everyone he meets) without wanting something from me, I would have laughed and let out a surly, "Yeah, right." But this look of love would still be a long-time coming. I see now that God's timing was perfect.

The Journey Begins

To leave the hospital after my drug overdose, I had to call my family. Because I made the call on my birthday, this eased the awkwardness of contacting my mother. I was out of the hospital, but I was still a mess, so I agreed to a friend's recommendation to speak with her Lutheran pastor. I'm sure it shocked many of his parishioners when I pulled up to the small church on my motorcycle. The pastor talked to me about Christianity, but as a dizzy twenty-six-year-old, I heard little more than a monotonous babble of "church talk." He asked me, "If you were to die tonight, do you know for sure you would go to heaven?" He seemed taken aback when I replied, "I couldn't care less."

He said that I needed to begin participating in a Bible study, but such an idea had little appeal to me. In the end, though, my friend Sheila convinced me to attend. She was afraid that if I didn't do something positive in my life, the next time I tried to kill myself I would succeed.

I attended the Bible study for several months and then was invited to join another Bible study made up of young adults, an invitation I accepted. The study met at a home in Taylor Ridge, Illinois, in the Quad Cities area. Despite my initial impression that this large group of young adults was a bunch of "goody-goodies," I quickly had a change of heart after experiencing their genuine faith and goodness. Later that night, I asked Jesus to help me know Him, and I made a commitment to live for Him.

Over the next few months, I got to know Otis and DeAnne Anderson, the couple who hosted the Bible study. They invited me to stay with them until I got back on my feet. My decision to accept their offer is likely the most pivotal decision I have ever made in my life. Although it did not happen overnight, God turned my life around. I changed my appearance, stopped using profanity, and softened my heart toward God and others. These changes were not easy for me. The Andersons put up with a lot during the two years I lived with them. How generous they were! Despite the challenges of raising five children, they took me in as if I were family. Being loved so openly was a challenge. I was a bit like an animal that, after being beaten for many years, cowers with fear when its new owner simply goes to pat it on the head.

After two years, I left the Andersons' home to attend an evangelical Christian Bible school in Texas with a member of the Bible study who had formed a youth outreach called the Mark IV Youth Ministry. The Bible training school was run by David Wilkerson, the author of the Christian classic *The Cross and the Switchblade.* By the time I arrived at his place in 1979, Wilkerson was well-known throughout the world. His book had been made into a movie starring Pat Boone and a young Eric Estrada, who would go on to star in the popular '70s TV show *CHiPs.*

Brother Dave, as we called him, was as gracious as a host could be. In time, he and his wife, Gwen, invited me to live with their family and to serve as Gwen's assistant. After three months or so, the leaders of Mark IV invited me to join them in their ministry. I believed in their ministry and in them, and I very much wanted to accept their offer. Brother Dave, though, strongly counseled against the move, as he had come to believe that the group was a cult. He was concerned that the ground I had gained in my walk with the Lord would be lost, and he offered to help me find another ministry. At the time, I didn't accept his negative view of Mark IV, and I decided to travel with the group.

I soon discovered that Brother Dave had been right. The leaders of Mark IV had us engaged in constant evangelism. We traveled in groups of two and weren't allowed any contact with family and friends. After getting caught writing a letter to the Andersons, I was harshly chastised. Initially, I saw this correction as a sign of their love and concern for me. After repeated emotional violations of my dignity, however, I left and moved back in with DeAnne and Otis. They convinced me to enroll in college and to again pursue a relationship with my family. I began my studies at Concordia University in suburban Chicago in the fall of 1980.

I was then thirty years old and still extremely overweight. In desperation, I resolved to stop eating. This would begin a cycle of binging and purging that would go on for the next twenty years, all in an attempt to alter my appearance. Little did I realize that it was my inward image that needed reconstructive surgery. The one great consolation from this period is that I graduated from Concordia with a degree in sociology.

Shortly after graduating, I met a man named Robert[1] at bar owned by Chicago Bear great Walter Payton. It was just minutes before midnight on New Year's Eve of 1985. I don't know whether it was the euphoria of the pre-midnight moment or my low self-esteem, but we hit it off instantly. Four days later, we were engaged; two weeks later, we were living with each other.

Robert was Catholic, and I started attending church with him shortly after we started living together. (Somehow, I didn't see any conflict between my Christian faith and engaging in premarital sex.) I believed that if we were going to be married, we needed to attend the same church. Eight months later, we were married in the Catholic Church.

Our marriage lasted nearly twenty years. As impressive as this was on one level, our relationship was seriously dysfunctional on almost all other levels. Robert viewed me as inferior and, as a result, he was demanding and controlling. Hard as I tried, I could never live up to his standards.

At various points during our marriage, I was consuming as much as 15,000 to 20,000 calories a day, only to purge them shortly after eating. Though I continued to struggle with bulimia throughout our marriage, Robert repeatedly denied my requests for counseling. In hindsight, I believe he allowed me to struggle with this problem

---

[1] Name has been changed.

because it was a warped way for him to control me. I couldn't fight him because he was the breadwinner of the family.

During the early years of our marriage, I was a "double dipper" when it came to church attendance. On Saturday night, we would attend the local Catholic parish, and on Sundays I would attend Willow Creek, the well-known mega-church in the Chicago area. When I traveled, I would attend various Protestant churches; I could never bring myself to engage in "Catholic stuff" when I wasn't with Robert. In fact, during my trips to other churches, I would spend a fair amount of time trying to get Catholics to become Protestant. Even in our Catholic parish, I used the forum of the Bible study to make the participants question their allegiance to the Church. I wanted to make sure they were really "saved," and I believed this was certain only if they prayed the Sinner's Prayer. Attending Mass was a bit of a ruse—done for spousal unity rather than real belief.

Robert and I moved to Colorado in 1996 so that he could attend law school. We searched out several Catholic churches and finally settled on St. Thomas Aquinas Parish in Boulder. After being at the parish for about seven years, I heard a homily by the associate pastor, Father David Dwyer, in which he used the phrase "Catholic Christian." I later e-mailed him, stating that this phrase was an oxymoron because "everyone knows that Catholics aren't really Christians." He sent me a lengthy reply that was filled with verses from the Bible explaining and defending Catholic teaching. I was blown away; I didn't think a Catholic priest could quote Scripture so skillfully. Not long after, we met and he corrected my misconceptions about the Catholic Church and its teachings. I was embarrassed at how closed to the Church my mind had been for so many years.

In 2003, I was received into the Catholic Church and accepted all the Church's teachings—except certain moral issues, which I would wrestle with for a few more years. I was confirmed by Archbishop Charles Chaput of Denver, and Father Dave was my sponsor. (Father Dave would soon move to New York to become the director of BustedHalo.com, a young adult outreach of the Paulist Fathers, and a radio host on Sirius satellite radio.)

Discovering the Theology of the Body

My parish, St. Thomas, is located near the University of Colorado. Several college friends of mine from St. Thomas began attending a Theology of the Body study group at a nearby parish, Sacred Heart of Mary, that was led by a young woman named Jamila Spencer. They related to me how amazing the Theology of the Body is, encouraging me to experience it for myself. I eventually went to one of the group's sessions just to observe. I was amazed to see college students so enthusiastic about teachings on morality (which is how I viewed the Theology of the Body at first). I was intrigued, so I listened to some talks by Christopher West on CD—but I fought the message almost the entire way.

Since I had such a poor image of myself, I struggled greatly with the idea that "the body was very good." Because of my sordid sexual past, I had difficulty with the lofty ideas that sex is beautiful and that a man could actually avoid lusting after a woman. Lust seemed like a normal part of life. In fact, it seemed to me a positive good, since it enabled people to get together. Of course, I came to understand that sexual attraction is much different from lust. Lust involves using another for one's selfish ends, whereas sexual attraction, when properly ordered toward the good of the other, is a God-given gift for which we should be thankful. Nevertheless, I struggled with the idea that I could live a life of holiness in light of the bad choices of my past.

Then came the issue of contraception. To me, using contraception was as normal as using any other modern convenience. I listened as West explained the logic of the Church's teaching, but I fought it, arguing about this and other issues with the group leader and then privately with the Lord. To me, it seemed logical that every man and woman engaged in sex should use contraception to avoid bringing unwanted children into the world. I reasoned that such children would be abused and then become abusers themselves. In light of the abuse in my past, I guess I could hardly be blamed for this thinking. (I also believed in the right to abortion, since many friends in my past had had one or more.)

At the time, I thought that Pope John Paul II was full of lofty ideas and wanted us to believe them so that, when we failed, we would be dependant on the Catholic Church. But a part of me wanted to believe in the Theology of the Body. I wanted to believe that "in the beginning," the world did not operate with a paradigm of lust and that we were created with an original beauty. I wanted to love myself and to believe that I could "see and be seen" by another and be loved purely for the sake of being loved. My heart longed for this experience, but my clouded mind told me that it was a pipe dream and that, because of my appearance and my past, no one would ever love me.

Pope John Paul II has said that "a man's interior life affirms the objective truth." Because my interior life was so messed up, I had trouble seeing what was normal and what was abnormal. According to John Paul, "experiences are always at the root of who we are," and we are often closed to these teachings because of our sinfulness. But he also offered hope by saying that, despite this sinfulness, we are "open to the mystery of redemption." The openness to the mystery must have been enough.

Being a slow learner and becoming ever more intrigued with the concepts of the Theology of the Body, I joined the study group again the following season. I can still remember being amazed when I learned about John Paul II's teaching on the "virginal experience." Initially, I thought the idea of virginity was quaint and not applicable to used and abused people like me. Just as a person could not return to his or her mother's womb, I thought that one cannot regain his or her virginity. But I learned that the virginity spoken of by the pope was rooted in an integrity of body and soul. The idea that a spiritually-restored virginity was possible through God's grace changed my life. I now had a basis on which I could allow God to heal the wounds of my life. I wasn't doomed by being a victim of my past. I had the chance to become whole.

The Theology of the Body also began to affect how I viewed other people. I started seeing others for who they were, not for what they were going to do for me—or to me. Acquiring this perspective, of course, took time and grace, but my hunger for this new way of thinking and living kept me moving forward. Love also took on new meaning. I wanted to love and to be loved, but before I could love others rightly, I had to first learn to love God. I still saw Him as one who loved us only if we did things just right.

What I ultimately learned through the Theology of the Body was that God's love was totally unconditional. Once this set in, I could begin to believe that others—my family, my friends, my pastor—could have the same kind of love. I marveled when I heard the quote about God's nature from the *Catechism*, "God has revealed his innermost secret: God himself is an eternal exchange of love, Father, Son, Holy Spirit, and He has destined us to share in that exchange." Imagine that! We are called to participate *in the very inner life of God!*

Redeemed and On Fire

To be redeemed from one's past is to believe in one's heart the promises of God and to live in a spirit of hope. I have gone on to lead Theology of the Body study groups, including one for teenagers. This outreach is near and dear to me because of my life as a teen. I so want to help these teens see the beautiful truth of their bodies and their sexuality before they are wounded by premarital sex.

In both my adult and teen sessions, I have heard many stories of why people come to take the class and how their lives have changed because of it. Many have changed their whole mindset on sexual issues, especially their previously entrenched acceptance of contraception. They no longer look at sex as a physical urge to be fulfilled but as a power to fulfill our deepest longings. Usually about halfway through the series, one can see the lights going on in the minds of the participants. They begin to see a whole new set of possibilities—ways to live life in a manner that brings about authentic freedom. One particular joy is to see the renewal of relationships between husbands and wives that has come from these sessions. The Theology of the Body can make monumental changes in our lives if we allow the truths within it to blossom in our hearts.

My life today is far from perfect. I know it won't be until I see Jesus face-to-face, but I understand now why we are called to strive for holiness here on earth. Not only does this holiness prepare us for eternity, but it also brings peace in the here and now. As one whose early life was traumatic, I find this peace attractive, to be sure. Through the Theology of the Body I have learned how to love and to forgive others and myself. I hope to continue to lead classes in the Theology of the Body and to help those who are afflicted gain back their inherent dignity. I will be thankful along the way should God allow me to witness the lives changed through this glorious teaching. In the meantime, I will simply give thanks for the profound renewal God has granted me in my own life.

Becoming the Father
I Had Been Called to Be

Fr. James Otto

I have come to believe that the current crisis of the shortage of priests in the West is rooted in a crisis of authentic masculinity. Due to a woefully deficient understanding in the culture of "who man is to be for woman and who woman is to be for man," to use the words of Pope John Paul II, the crisis of masculinity also has hit the Catholic priesthood, resulting in a substantial drop in the number of vocations in the past thirty years. In addition, it has fueled a culture of sexual "dis-integration" with many of our clergy.

Until we reclaim the rich understanding of authentic masculinity found in the Scripture and in the writings of the great mystics, we will be a Church filled with men who struggle with sexual sin and with a sizable percentage of priests who have simply learned to cope with—rather than truly live out—the gift of their sexuality.

Having dated in high school, I struggled with the idea of the celibate life after I experienced a rich renewal of my Catholic faith following college. Like many men who experience such a conversion, the possibility that I was being called to be a priest occurred to me. Heart-stopping moments when I reflected on the totality of this commitment followed. Sure, the chivalry and sacrificial aspects of the priesthood are attractive, but at some point the reality of the seriousness of such a call demands an answer.

During my seminary years, I had moments when I felt certain about my vocation. Nonetheless, while I was on retreat before my third year of theological studies, the question "Can I do this?" hit me hard. This year would culminate in my ordination to the diaconate—and my commitment to the celibate life.

I remember talking to two of my brother seminarians the night before we left the retreat. I was describing my fears, concerns, and doubts about my ability to live and be happy in the celibate vocation. The next morning, I was in the parking lot waiting for the shuttle to the airport. Father Bill Gaffney, C.Ss.R., was with me. In the middle of our small talk, something powerful happened. Father Gaffney began to prophesy, a gift that he is known to exhibit on occasion. Father Gaffney repeated to me exactly what I had said to my brother seminarians concerning my fears and doubts about the celibate vocation. He had no natural knowledge of my fears in this area or of the conversation that I had had the night before. After restating my concerns, he reaffirmed that the Lord was calling me to be a priest— that He was calling me to stay close to Him in the Eucharist and to Mary, and to make frequent use of the sacrament of reconciliation.

His reassuring counsel was an extraordinary gift. To this day, I believe that God had spoken to me through this humble and holy priest. Though I didn't make my promise of celibacy until my diaconate ordination ten months later, I made a definitive surrender in my heart then and there. Little did I know that my understanding of the glory of the priesthood, of God's plan for man and woman, and of living a life of sexual integration had only just begin. My understanding of these issues would hit "warp speed" after I was introduced to the Theology of the Body through the works of Catholic philosopher Dr. Janet Smith.

Understanding and Integrating This Teaching

Early in my seminary studies, I came to understand the fundamental change in how the laity and much of the clergy viewed the Church since the 1968 release of Pope Paul VI's encyclical *Humanae Vitae*, which reaffirmed the intrinsic immorality of contraception. The Church has been deeply wounded by the dissent from *Humanae Vitae*, which continues to the present day. The enemy's lies about the truth and meaning of sexuality and of marital intercourse have held the Church in bondage. Rather than transforming the culture, many in the Church were being transformed by the culture—a culture that would soon be powerfully affected by the sexual revolution.

In reading the works of Janet Smith, particularly *Humanae Vitae: A Generation Later* and *Why Humanae Vitae Was Right: A Reader*, I learned about the Theology of the Body and some of its key concepts. Like many, I was instantly captivated by both its grounding in tradition and its fresh approach to perennial questions of sex, human desire, and the meaning of our existence. I came to see that this revolutionary theology was a powerful antidote to the ills of our modern culture. I felt called to study these issues more deeply so I took a concentration of elective courses in moral theology.

Despite the richer intellectual conversion I was experiencing, I knew that life as a celibate priest would not be a cakewalk. I did not fully understand the gift of celibacy that I was being offered, and I naturally wondered how I would live a happy, fulfilled integrated life without a wife.

As my study deepened, I came to see the Theology of the Body as an instrument of salvation and sanctification for leading souls to offer their bodies to God in an act of spiritual worship (Romans 12:1). This offering of one's body culminates on earth in "nuptial union" with the Divine Beloved as a rich foretaste of the blissful spousal union of God and man in heaven. John Paul II spoke often of this nuptial or spousal union as a key insight in understanding our relationship with God.

In the Theology of the Body, Pope John Paul II invites married couples to experience their marriage and their marital intercourse as two persons wholly possessed by this Divine Beloved. He goes on to describe what this union looks like and how we can reach these summits. Through this teaching, the pope also invites celibates to sacrifice the taste of heaven on earth—that is, marital intercourse—to instead experience union with the Divine Beloved on earth in anticipation of the union they will eternally and ecstatically possess with Him at the Wedding Feast of the Lamb.

Such language gave me an even greater understanding of and attraction to my priestly vocation. Although I will always have a certain longing for married life and the natural goods that come with it, this newly infused understanding of celibacy for the sake of the Bride, the Church, was sufficient to guide me through ordination and into my early years of priesthood. This higher level of understanding and integration of my calling to the celibate life came through the Theology of the Body. In 1997, I was ordained to the priesthood, and my life married to the Church began in earnest.

The Twisting of the Good—and the Untwisting

It has traditionally been understood that biblical passages have multiple, layered meanings and symbolisms. In Ephesians 5:31-32, for example, St. Paul speaks of the one-flesh union as a "great mystery" and then equates it to Christ and the Church. In sacrificial love, Christ, the Bridegroom, gave up His body for His Bride, the Church—which is reflected in the Mass when the priest says, "This is my body, given up for you." In the same way, a husband and wife give up their respective bodies in the marital act, and the result is often a great sacrifice, both emotional and physical, through the begetting of new life.

Marital intercourse is an act of worship, inasmuch as the couple allows the sacrament of Christ to be made present in the sacrament of the Bridegroom and the Bride. Just as the Mass represents the one sacrifice of Jesus on the cross, so, too, do couples receive again the grace received at the altar when they committed themselves to each other freely, totally, faithfully, and fruitfully.

This profound understanding of the marital act served as an additional source of grace for my understanding of my vocation as a priest. Instead of seeing my sexuality as something I was "giving up" in living a celibate life, I came to see it as an extraordinary participation in God's divine plan to "marry us" in a mystical sense, as St. John of the Cross contends. I began to appreciate that I am metaphysically marrying the Church each day when I again give my consent to the priesthood. And, in particular, standing *in persona Christi* ("in the person of Christ"), I give up my body when I celebrate the Holy Sacrifice of the Mass. This understanding soon began to have a profoundly positive effect on my marriage preparation efforts with engaged couples—especially in how I presented the Church's vision for human sexuality and marriage.

Healing through Christ's Masculinity and the Eucharist

After I had been ordained for a few years, two things began to happen simultaneously. In my own parish and beyond, I was given opportunities to share the Theology of the Body with friends, parishioners, and engaged couples. I began to see hearts opened and transformed. The Theology of the Body also continued to transform my understanding of the celibate vocation and of myself.

In the summer of 2000, I met Christopher West for the first time at a Couple to Couple League Convention. I found his presentation to be powerful, and I was hungry for more. I began a study of the Eucharist and its relation to the Theology of the Body.

Being a student of the great mystics in our Catholic tradition (who were in touch with the imagery and ideas of "mystical marriage" with God) prepared me to appreciate some fascinating Christian art I discovered. Up to this point, I'd had no idea that an entire genre of Catholic art from the Middle Ages, commonly embraced by the Church and the masses, presented the human body in an overt but tasteful manner. Some readers may have encountered such art, whether it be the Blessed Mother with her breast exposed nursing the infant Jesus, or St. Teresa of Avila in ecstasy, or even images of Christ naked on the cross.

These were not the lustful sacrileges of Martin Scorsese's film *The Last Temptation of Christ.* The artist's intent was not to incite lust or to focus salaciously on the body. Rather, these classic works communicated a deeper mystery of the human person to a world that was substantially more in touch with the goodness of the body. Such artwork brought about healing and transformed my understanding of the priesthood and myself.

I came to understand that Jesus had what it took to be physically fruitful, which was necessary for His spiritual fruitfulness. On the cross, Jesus was the sacramental sign of the Father's potency. And it is a sacramental principle that sacramental signs convey what they signify. Jesus' potent masculine body was the necessary sacramental sign of the Father's potency and fruitfulness.

Because our culture idolizes sexual activity, this new vision of the body was healing for me in my masculine identity as a celibate priest. In calling me to be celibate, Jesus was not calling me to be less of a man but rather more of a man. He had called and was calling me to sacrifice marriage, marital relations, and biological children so that I could enter all the more into His potent, fruitful, masculine gift of self on the cross.

At this time in my priesthood, it seemed that the Lord was going to open the door for me to be able to share the Theology of the Body as my primary ministerial assignment. As Blessed Teresa of Calcutta once said, though, if you want to make God laugh, tell Him your plans. The moment I thought I was gearing up for Theology of the Body ministry, I was sent to an assignment for which I did not feel at all prepared.

In the summer of 2000, I was assigned as a full-time faculty member at St. John Neumann High School for boys in South Philadelphia. Though I saw many wonderful things happen at Neumann, it was a difficult experience. Through it, though, I was led to go deeper into my understanding of the Theology of the Body, in terms of how to share it and how to live it. During an extended summer retreat after my second year at Neumann, the Lord gave me profound insights into the riches of this revolutionary teaching.

In my seminary years and after ordination, I had had the good fortune of going on several retreats with the Intercessors of the Lamb, a devout religious community that specializes in spiritual warfare. Led by Mother Nadine Brown, the Intercessors focus on the healing of a person's wounds—spiritual, emotional, and psychological. One of the exercises prescribed is the ancient practice of *lectio divina*, in which one prays deeply using Sacred Scripture, asking the Lord for guidance and understanding.

During one period in which the Lord was healing past memories, a memory came to mind from my seminary days in which celibacy, sexuality, and, specifically, nocturnal emissions ("wet dreams") were being discussed. (Again, I do not mean to scandalize anyone. During the preparation of men for the priesthood, prudence requires that issues of sexuality be addressed. Since seminarians are "normal" men, they will at times experience such biological realities as nocturnal emissions. Addressing such issues contributes to the integration of the sexual gift to which all Catholics are called. We need not fear the body or its natural processes. Written into the body are truths—eternal truths—that, when properly understood, can lead to a healthy, integrated living out of the gift.)

I recall one instance in the seminary when a particular priest said that if a seminarian or priest were "pure enough," he would not have wet dreams. Perhaps I didn't hear him accurately, but these words were lodged in my mind. At this point in my priesthood, this memory negatively affected my understanding of my masculinity, my celibate vocation, and myself.

I began to think about the implications of this statement. If a seminarian or a priest were not engaged in releasing his semen through masturbation or some other sin, how was it being released from his body, other than through nocturnal emissions? If I were "pure enough," would I no longer produce sperm and semen? Would my body still produce testosterone? Would those parts which identify me as a man function at all?

In this healing prayer, the Lord showed me that I had been hit with an angelistic lie. As Pope John Paul II points out in the Theology of the Body, we need to avoid two erroneous responses to human sexuality: angelism (in which we embrace the false, even heretical, notion that the "things of the spirit are good" and "those of the body are evil") and animalism (with its nearly inordinate focus on the body to the detriment of all things spiritual).

Authentic Catholic teaching stresses the need for a proper integration of the good of the sexual gift with its proper ordering in our lives. The notion that if a celibate man were "pure enough" the normal physical dimensions of his masculinity would no longer function is simply false. The net effect of this angelistic lie was that I felt cut off from the psychological, emotional, and spiritual potency of masculinity.

During this same retreat, the Lord brought to mind another memory from my seminary formation on the same topic. In this case, the priest was a well-known national figure. With a wry smile, he told us that if a celibate man has a sexual dream that he is not responsible for bringing on—by viewing inappropriate material before bed, for example—he should "just enjoy the dream." While the words of the other priest had been an angelistic lie, what this priest had said had an animalistic dimension.

Jesus began to show me that He wanted to transform and integrate my masculinity and my understanding of the celibate vocation even on a subconscious level, even on the level of what I may experience in dreams. Jesus didn't want my dreams to be just a place where disordered and unintegrated sexual desires could be safely expressed and released; He wanted to integrate me and transform me on this level of my being.

Singing the Priestly Song

The Song of Songs is the book of the Bible that reveals to us, in beautiful imagery, the love to which men and women are called. It also offers an analogy of God's love for humanity, which may explain why the great saints and mystics commented more on it than on any other book. As Pope John Paul II teaches in the Theology of the Body, the Song is a beautiful lyrical celebration of the one-flesh union of sacramental marriage. Mystically, the Song is sung between Jesus, the Bridegroom, and His bride, the Church.

Pope John Paul II said, "The Eucharist is the sacrament of the Bridegroom and the Bride." Thus, in the Incarnation, the flesh that the Word took on was male. Jesus' masculine body symbolizes the gift of the redemption that He initiates, and a woman's feminine body symbolizes the receptivity that every person is called to have in response to Jesus' "masculine" gift.

It was one thing for me to understand all this on an intellectual level. That was safe. But when the Lord began to open up the Song on an experiential level—as the song between the Bridegroom and the Bride—I was a little disconcerted. I had to go through a series of healings on that retreat so that I could be open to the deep union with Jesus that He offers to each of us.

I remember clearly one of these healings. As I was praying before the Blessed Sacrament, the Lord brought to mind something a well-known Catholic speaker had said. At the end of one of his talks, he recommended several books. One of these was about Jesus, and it was entitled *This Tremendous Lover.* Before he recommended this book, though, he put out a disclaimer: He said that the book was wonderful in spite of the fact that its title was a bit off the mark. His clear implication was that referring to Jesus as a "lover" was inappropriate.

While it was not clear to me what this well-respected Catholic presenter's concern was on this point, his comment stirred up the lingering insecurities I had regarding my masculinity. How was I, a man with normal, heterosexual desires, supposed to view Christ? Did my masculine posture toward Christ allow me to see Him in only masculine terms, such as a savior or spiritual warrior? Thankfully, in prayer, Jesus showed me that what was true of me was what was true of every male member of the Church throughout history. Those who were the most "masculine" (i.e., potent) were precisely those who were the most "feminine" (i.e., receptive) with regard to the Bridegroom. In other words, the influential men in Church history—the saints and mystics—were the ones who knew and experienced Jesus as Bridegroom.

Jesus began to show me that He was so powerful in His masculinity because He was, first of all, completely receptive ("feminine") in His relationship with the Father. He began to show me that the Song was, first of all, a Song of the eternal love between the Father and the Son, with the Son as the Bride and the Father as the Bridegroom. Our fallen world, with its distorted views of sexuality, can see such a posture (receptivity towards Christ) only in a fallen, eroticized manner. There is so much more to see.

The breakthroughs of the head and heart that I experienced with this new perspective opened me up to receive gifts of contemplative prayer. These gifts have been wonderfully overwhelming. I began to feel that the following section of Pope John Paul II's *Novo Millennio Ineunte* was personally addressed to me:

> But we who have received the grace of believing in Christ, the revealer of the Father and the Savior of the world, have a duty to show to what depths the relationship with Christ can lead. The great mystical tradition of the Church of both East and West has much to say in this regard. It shows how prayer can progress, as a genuine dialogue of love, to the point of rendering the person wholly possessed by the divine Beloved, vibrating at the Spirit's touch, resting filially within the Father's heart. This is the lived experience of Christ's promise: "He who loves me will be loved by my Father, and I will love him and manifest myself to him" (Jn 14:21). It is a journey totally sustained by grace, which nonetheless demands an intense spiritual commitment and is no stranger to painful purifications (the "dark night"). But it leads, in various possible ways, to the ineffable joy experienced by the mystics as "nuptial union." How can we forget here, among the many shining examples, the teachings of Saint John of the Cross and Saint Teresa of Avila? (no. 33).

I began to hunger and thirst for deeper and deeper levels of union with the Bridegroom. At the same time, something was happening to me and to my priesthood. People were beginning to say things like "your preaching is so life-giving." As I was becoming more receptive (more "feminine") to the Bridegroom, I also was becoming more potent, more "masculine," as a priest.

I also was beginning to see that I was called to a special marriage-preparation ministry. The Bridegroom was bringing to me souls who were seeking, through spiritual direction, to experience "nuptial union" with the Bridegroom. I was being asked as spiritual director to be involved in an important marriage preparation indeed—the preparation of believers for the mystical marriage we will all have with God in eternity.

The Theology of the Body is, to be sure, a powerful weapon of spiritual warfare. It also is a powerful tool for opening doors to sexual integration and to mystical union with the Bridegroom. I am grateful for this opportunity to thank Pope John Paul II, and each of the Persons of the Trinity, who have been gracious in bestowing these gifts on me. Through Pope John Paul II's intercession, may all receive the grace to pursue deeper and deeper levels of sexual integration and mystical union with the Bridegroom, the Father, and the Holy Spirit, in this world and the next.

Father James Otto currently serves as the pastor of St. Ignatius of Loyola Parish in Philadelphia.

Breaking the Chains of Sex
and Secular Humanism

Jesse Romero

I lied to my wife on our wedding day.

When Anita and I professed our vows in front of a large group of family and friends at the historic San Fernando Mission Church on May 21, 1983, I promised to "accept children lovingly." In truth, I never intended to have kids, but I said the words "I do" anyway. Beginning in the early days of our marriage, I repeatedly told my wife that I did not want to be a father. I even told her that if she got pregnant, I would walk out on her. Today, I think back on those words with shame and sorrow. I had not known that I was crushing the rose I had been given.

In essence, I wanted to be a "married single." I wanted to indulge in sports, exercise, sex, vacations, and a healthy bank account without the "burden" of children. My models were the people I saw on TV who "had it all" and seemed happy. If anyone ever had a case for an annulment, it was my wife. Yet, instead of walking out on me, Anita remained faithful to the vows she had made and believed. She also sought solace in her two mothers—her earthly one and her heavenly one, Mary, as she stormed heaven for many years with her prayers for my conversion.

Thanks to God's grace, my conversion came—in several waves

and with deeper levels of intensity, as I began to "fight the good fight" of which St. Paul speaks. Today, my life's work is as a lay evangelist, apologist, and catechist. I can bear witness to how glorious are God's truth and grace. Every time I read a book, listen to a speaker, or receive the Eucharist, I am reminded of the great gifts God gives each of us —even hardheaded and hard-hearted persons like the "me" of years past.

The latest mind-blowing reality to which God has opened my heart is the collection of works known as the Theology of the Body. Since my "awakening" to Christianity in 1987 and return to Catholicism in 1989, I have experienced many extraordinary gifts of God. I am here to say, though, that the ramifications of the TOB for my faith are incalculable. In a nutshell, the integration of "body and spirit" that this Christian synthesis offers has, in many ways, vivified all aspects of my life because it is the Catholic sacramental worldview—on steroids. (More on this a little later.) I will share a bit more about my background to illustrate the impact that TOB has had on my life.

Where the "Culture of Death" Was Normalized

In a recent World Youth Day homily, Pope Benedict XVI implored young people to "discover the beauty of love ... not a disposable love that is transient and deceptive, imprisoned in a selfish and materialistic mindset, but true, deep love." I wish such words had penetrated my heart as a Hispanic teenager growing up in 1970s Southern California. I was a disciple of the opposite worldview, one that saw love as disposable.

I was raised in the San Fernando Valley by Catholic immigrant parents from Mexico who never talked to their children about "the birds and the bees." Such topics were taboo in my Latino culture. What I didn't learn from my parents I learned from the media, my teachers, and my peers. It also didn't help that more than ninety percent of the world's pornography was produced and shipped just ten minutes from my home. In addition, subtle moral manipulations assaulted the sensibilities of my friends and me via the freeway billboards, convenience-store magazines, and values-free sex education in public school. These influences set me on a destructive path from which I almost never turned back.

My generation was taught to be the arbiters of truth. In our schools, we learned to question authority, relying instead on our subjective feelings and the growing trend of "values clarification." I remember clearly sitting in Mr. Crowell's Values Awareness class and witnessing the conservative beliefs of my parents go up in smoke. In the case of some of my friends, that smoke was literal (and illegal).

I never heard a lecture in a religion class or a homily at church on human sexuality or God's glorious plan for sex. The idea of abstinence never crossed my mind or the minds of the guys I hung out with. I didn't hear of Natural Family Planning (NFP) until I was nearly thirty, when I returned to the practice of my Catholic faith. My only exposure to "responsible" messages about sex came from my public school curriculum. The message, though, was that we are all higher-level animals whose sexual choices are morally neutral. And if people happened to have a difficult time controlling their sexual urges, they would find greater happiness in indulging rather than repressing them. The "use a condom" mantra came across as dogma to my high school peers.

From Karate to Cop to Cultural Catholic

My life took an interesting turn when I was twelve years old. I discovered karate and latched on to it with a vengeance. Despite some of the "New Age" ideas that came through in my classes, karate became one of the stabilizing forces in my life. For the next nine years, I worked hard and progressed to fairly high levels in the sport, achieving my black belt and winning a number of championships.

The discipline that karate gave me paved the way for a career in law enforcement. At twenty-one, I joined the Los Angeles County Sheriff's Department, not because I had idealistic motives but because the image of a deputy sheriff in Los Angeles was sharp and professional. I remember looking at a billboard advertisement for the program and thinking, "I want to be on that winning team. They look like they are in control."

I loved my time in the academy. After a twelve-hour day, I would go home, shine my shoes and leather gear, and study my manuals for another hour or two. This enthusiasm stayed with me during my eighteen years on the force. I knew from the start that I wanted to be a deputy sheriff—a "street cop"—and not a "suit" who rose in the ranks by working behind a desk.

My work in law enforcement thrust me into LA's infamous gang culture. I witnessed some of the worst acts of humanity possible. I saw firsthand the ravages of prostitution on women and of drug use on otherwise "normal" working-class people. I held in my arms people dying from stab or gunshot wounds. It is no wonder that, as a person with little faith, I would say to my wife repeatedly, "There's no way I want to bring a child into this violent, corrupt world." In many areas of my life, I was an optimist, but when it came to the idea of raising children, I was jaded and pessimistic. My wife, in emotional pain, would just sigh, realizing that she could end up childless. Her knight in shining armor was falling down at this most important post.

A few years ago, I read Sheldon Vanauken's masterwork *A Severe Mercy*. In the book, Vanauken speaks of the love that he and his wife shared. It was a powerful, pagan love, beautiful but devoid of the sacrificial, agape love to which Christian marriage aspires. As a lukewarm Catholic, I still retained a certain idea of human love, but it was riddled with selfishness. In the Theology of the Body, we learn that spousal (i.e., marital) love is an icon of God's love for us, a foreshadowing of the union we will have with God in heaven. If God's love is our destination, then human love is the "road sign" that points us toward the destination we desire. As theologian Christopher West points out in his talks and books, problems arise when we turn the icon into an idol. Such was the case early in my marriage to Anita. Our love was beautiful and true, but I had made this love the end rather than the means to union with God.

In terms of my faith, I fell into the category of a cultural Catholic. I viewed Jesus as little more than an important moral figure in history, certainly not as the Lord who was calling me to a relationship with Him. The idea of having a personal relationship with God struck me as hokey—something that the old ladies who sat in the front of church during Mass would care about.

Two Bible verses from the first chapter of St. Paul's letter to the Romans described me perfectly: "For although they knew God they did not honor him as God or give thanks to him, but they became futile in their thinking and their senseless minds were darkened" (v. 21). "And since they did not see fit to acknowledge God, God gave them up to a base mind and to improper conduct" (v. 28). I attended Sunday Mass out of habit, not conviction.

The Turning Point—and Then a Surprise

Not surprisingly, after four years of living as a "married single," I began to feel empty. There was a vacuum in my life, and my marriage was not filling it. I was restless, not at peace. By this point, I had become friends with a fellow officer named Paul Clay. He was a likable guy who, despite the violence and brutality he and I witnessed every day on the streets, was at peace with himself and the world. One day, he casually shared that he was a Christian. As the weeks went by, he gradually shared more of his Christian faith, and I found that I was open to what he was saying—even though much of it contradicted the little I knew about my own faith.

Over the next few months, I began seriously to read and study the Bible, but I was being guided by Protestant teachers. I had always believed that the Bible was the Word of God, but now, as I read it for myself, I felt that God was directly speaking to my heart. Slowly, God was scraping away all the barnacles of secular thought that had attached to my soul over the years. Though I was still going to Mass with my wife, I also began to attend my friend Paul's evangelical Christian services. I still would have claimed to be a Catholic at this point, but I had embraced evangelical Christian beliefs about the Bible, salvation, and the nature of the Church. By default, I had started to question many Catholic doctrines.

About two years into this reawakening of my Christian faith, another friend, Danny Miramontes, gave me an audiotape of a former Presbyterian minister, Scott Hahn, who had recently become Catholic.

I was floored at what I heard in his testimony. I soon became convinced that my newfound Protestant leanings were misguided in a number of key areas. In short order, my misconceptions about Catholicism were corrected. I had begun my journey back to the Catholic faith.

Dr. Hahn's conversion was fueled, in part, by his Presbyterian wife Kimberly's own study of the contraception issue. Kimberly had sufficiently convinced her husband that the Catholic Church's teaching on contraception was correct. As Dr. Hahn laid out the rationale for Christianity's long-standing prohibition against intentionally thwarting the procreative power of the sexual act, my interest was piqued. Needing some answers from a "biblical perspective," I ordered a book called *The Bible and Birth Control* by Charles Provan, a lay Protestant. The arguments against contraception from Scripture, as presented by Provan, and from Christian history and natural law, as outlined by Dr. Hahn, were extremely persuasive.

The Lord was beginning to remove the veil of darkness from my eyes—but I was not yet fully convinced. I shared what I was learning with Anita, and an amazing thing happened. A few days later, she went to the medicine cabinet, took out her birth control pills, and flushed them down the toilet. I watched in silence.

She turned around, looked at me, and said, "I had a feeling contraception was wrong, but now I *know* it's wrong. Never, ever again."

"But honey, can't we discuss this?" I pleaded.

"There is nothing to discuss. We will do what the Church teaches."

Anita was breathing fire, and I didn't dare cross her!

I soon came to see that our story was the story of millions of Catholics who had been led into a contraceptive mindset. Knowing now the serious social, spiritual, physical, and psychological effects of contraception—on the individual, on couples, and on society as a whole—I can't help conjuring up the image of "lambs being led to slaughter." Like so many, we had bought contraception hook, line, and sinker. It was as if we were stumbling in the dark without realizing that we were in the dark. As the renowned Fr. John Hardon, S.J., put it: "The single, principal cause for the breakdown of the Catholic faith in materially overdeveloped countries like ours has been contraception."[1] And Fr. Gabriel Amorth, chief exorcist for the Diocese of Rome, has said that the devil "tries every trick to force man's body to become an occasion for sin. [He] tries to humiliate the body, to break it, as a raging reaction against the incarnation of the Word, who, through his sacrificed Body, redeemed us."[2] The devil is anti-Church and anti-Christ, so "[he] uses the idolatry of sex, which reduces the human body to an instrument against sin."[3] I have come to believe that contraception is one of his greatest tricks.

Anita and I signed up for Natural Family Planning classes at a neighboring parish, and we began to buy all the materials on the topic we could lay our hands on. We read Pope Paul VI's landmark 1968 encyclical *Humanae Vitae (Of Human Life)* and a host of other works, including *Birth Control and Christian Discipleship*, by Dr. John Kippley. Of course, elements of Theology of the Body can be found in all of these works, though I was not aware of the Theology of the Body at the time.

As we began to delve deeper, one of the most shocking discoveries we made was that the birth control pill can sometimes work as an

[1]   See www.ewtn.com/library/Christ/confatal.txt
[2]   Gabriel Amorth, *An Exorcist Tells His Story*, p.197.
[3]   *Ibid.*, p. 29.

abortifacient. Despite the pill's intended purpose of suppressing ovulation, some eggs are still released over the course of a year and can be fertilized—thus leading to conception. An additional effect of the pill is to make the wall of the uterus inhospitable to the fertilized ovum during the time of implantation. In effect, the pill causes an early abortion. Anita and I have chosen to trust in God's unfathomable promise that He will not hold our sins against any children whom we may have conceived during this time. Scripture says that God will be a father to the fatherless and a father to the orphan (see Psalm 68:5). We believe by faith that they are now in heaven with our merciful Lord.

After Anita stopped taking the pill, it took nine months for her to become pregnant. From conversations we have had with experts in this area, we believe this was due to the overall polluting of the womb from the chemicals in the contraception. By God's grace, though, our firstborn, Paul, came into the world in 1989. Annmarie joined him in 1992 and Joshua in 1995. We have not been able to conceive more children since then. In retrospect, I believe that the pill had a lingering effect on her and eventually caused the infertility that we have experienced since after the birth of Joshua.

Discovering the Theology of the Body

After my return—in heart and mind—to the Church, I learned much about her teachings, including in the area of sexual ethics. I could argue the logic of why one should save sex for marriage and why contraception was immoral. Little did I know, though, that a new, rich understanding still lay ahead.

By the time the new millennium had rolled around, I was working full-time in Catholic ministry. I had just retired from the sheriff's department due to an on-the-job injury. Being in the field of Catholic ministry, I had heard of Theology of the Body sooner than most who work for the Church. Terry Barber, a friend of mine in ministry and the founder of St. Joseph Communications, had recorded Christopher West at a conference, stating that this theology was a "gold mine" of riches for the Church. The combination of the words "theology" and "body" sounded a bit strange, but then I quickly began to recall or notice Bible passages such as I Corinthians 3:16-17 and 6:19-20, which speak of our bodies as "temples of the Lord," and Genesis 1:28, which urges us "to be fruitful and multiply." These verses took on a new meaning.

The cylinders in my brain started firing, and I began to see the connection between the Theology of the Body and many aspects of the Catholic faith. In hindsight, this connection makes perfect sense because Pope John Paul II's work was intended, in part, to be a synthesis of Catholic theology. The Theology of the Body amplified the Catholic sacramental worldview, in which we see in God's revelation in the created order. It was an attempt by John Paul II to remove any false dualism—any overemphasis of either "body" or "spirit"—that may have crept into our understanding of God's creation, particularly the human person. It would take a creative and simple synthesis for the average Catholic to access the profound riches of the Theology of the Body.

After listening to Christopher West's presentation, my first thought was one rooted in a bit of Catholic pride. I thought, the world sees Pope John Paul II as just a celibate old man, yet he has taught the world, in a very gentle and fatherly way, the sublime truths of the human person and sexuality. I knew that these teachings had always been present in the Church, but the Lord used the particular gifts of this saintly pope to unpack and unveil them to a world in great need of their healing insights.

Over the next few years, I found myself speaking at a few conferences where Christopher was speaking. I also had picked up a series of his recordings and his book *Good News about Sex and Marriage*. My fascination with the Theology of the Body continued to increase. By this point, I had heard some criticism of Christopher's work, strangely enough, from "orthodox" Catholics, i.e., from those who strongly supported the Church's teaching. While Church history shows that this opposition is not uncommon when a new theological approach is put forth in the Church, I respected many of those who were issuing words of caution about Christopher's presentations. I think that those of us in the "orthodox Catholic" camp are—rightly or wrongly—a bit suspicious of anything "new" because we have seen many "innovations" that turned out to be aberrations, approaches that ended up denying essential Catholic teaching.

Wanting to gain a deeper understanding of the Theology of the Body so that I could incorporate its "pearls of great price" into my apologetic and catechetical teaching, I signed up for the weeklong Head and Heart Immersion Course offered by the Theology of the Body Institute. I had heard that the week would be intense, as we would be in class for more than thirty hours. It was that and more.

After my experience in the immersion course, I concluded that some Catholics misunderstood Christopher's presentation of the Theology of the Body—and, frankly, what the Church has historically taught on these sensitive issues. I have come to believe that a large number of traditional Catholics are uncomfortable with the body and sexuality. Many implicitly hold a Protestant, dualistic view of the world and the human person. They see the "things of the spirit" as good and holy, and the "things of the body" as fundamentally bad and corrupt. This is not the official Catholic view, which sees the body as seriously wounded by original sin but not totally corrupted; the body retains its essential goodness (Genesis 1:31). A chasm of difference separates these two worldviews, with profound implications on how Christians live their lives.

Seeing the Body Anew

After that extraordinary week, I needed a personal retreat to recharge my batteries. While I did get recharged, I also got fired up. I learned more than I had anticipated. I was reminded how far the world has drifted from the truth—especially the truth about human sexuality. In addition, I came to see that many Catholics have lost sight of the profound ramifications of Christ's Incarnation for all of Christian theology. I also came to see the wounds I had in my own heart from the choices I had made in the past, as well as the shortcomings in my theological understanding.

In addition, the Theology of the Body has been an antidote to the repressive mentality of my upbringing. Christ is not a policeman who came to enforce the law. Rather, He is a surgeon who changes the heart and purifies the gaze. Christ's redemption is effective; it is real power that gushes forth from the cross to set us free from sin (see Galatians 5:1). The Theology of the Body has redeemed and renewed my understanding of sexuality. Sex has become for me good, true, beautiful, and holy beyond words. Through the Theology of the Body, I have come to see that the Church teaches neither repression nor indulgence. When we repress our sexual desires, it is like putting a wild beast in a cage. We can shut up our desires for a time, but they remain wild. Self-mastery is not repressing the beast; it is transforming the beast. Concupiscence, the inclination to sin, is still there, but it doesn't control us.

The Theology of the Body also has helped me to see pornography for what it is. The sexual act reveals much more than the human body; it reveals the whole self. Correspondingly, the soul is touched as much in sex as the body is. Much of our secular society rejects that idea. To see the body as a whole is the goal of the redeemed man. Seeing the body in its isolated parts is the goal of pornography. Pornography does not integrate the body; it is a "dis-integration" of the body. According to Pope John Paul II, pornography does not show too much of the human person; it shows too little.

It is amazing that the addiction to pornography is an attempt to satisfy the ache for the infinite with the finite. The Theology of the Body is an evangelical tool for teaching modern man and woman their true destiny. Those who follow the "cult of the body" are people who, deep down, are looking for holiness. As G. K. Chesterton put it, every man who rings the bell at the brothel is unconsciously looking for God.[4] Once the patrons of pornography are taught to integrate the entire human person, they will see how they have been robbed by the likes of Playboy founder Hugh Hefner. Even the purveyors of pornography are searching for God. It is my prayer that they might come to know the Theology of the Body and be converted to the truth they are seeking in their misguided

---

4 Bruce Smith, *The World, the Flesh, and Father Smith* (1945), p.108. Available at http://chesterton.org/qmeister2/questions.htm

atry of the body. For "love is not an ascent from the beast, but a descent from Divinity."[5]

My relationship with Anita has taken a turn for the better. Through our encounter with this teaching, Anita and I have come to understand that we are called to be a gift to each other. A man is the priest of his home and a woman is the tabernacle, which means she should be seen as beautiful to the man. The Theology of the Body has opened my eyes to the majesty of woman, seeing her as an icon of all of humanity in her receptivity. I now approach Anita with more reverence and honor. I understand at a deeper level the powerful words of the Second Vatican Council: "Man, who is the only creature on earth which God willed for itself, cannot fully find himself except through a sincere gift of himself."[6]

This teaching has also transformed our marriage in much the same way that the love of Sheldon and Davy Vanauken was transformed in A Severe Mercy. When the Vanaukens entered into the journey of divine love, they encountered a love that far outweighed and outshone their love for one another. Their inspiring story demonstrates that, while love between humans can be wonderful and intense, divine love and longing for union with God are much more so. In like manner, the love my wife and I share became more purified once we opened our hearts to the Lord. At this stage in my life, I understand that my marriage is but a foretaste of my desire to be united to God. It is unfair to expect my wife to be my total fulfillment. That is impossible because the eternal plan for both of us is the "Marriage of the Lamb," spiritual union with God. As Bishop Sheen puts it, "Too many married people expect

---

[5] Fulton Sheen, *Three to Get Married* (1951), p. 200.

[6] *Gaudium et Spes*, no. 24

their partner to give that which only God can give, namely, an eternal ecstasy. If man or woman could give that which the heart wants, he or she would be God."[7]

As a former LA cop and kickboxer, I had a masculine modality. Yet in my relationship to God, I had no choice but to be receptive— because He is God and I am not. So this teaching has helped me appreciate that aspect of Catholicism. Catholic author Mark Shea once wrote in an article on Catholic Exchange that Protestantism is often attractive—especially to men—because its modality is masculine. Catholicism, on the other hand, with its sacramental life and devotions, is more "receptive" and thus incorporates the feminine as well. We can see this contrast in other subtle ways as well. For example, Catholics use the word "evangelization" to describe the process of spreading the Gospel message throughout the world. Evangelical Protestants, though, speak of "evangelism," which has the connotations of proselytism. It may sound like a small difference, but it bespeaks of a substantially different approach to faith, and it has ramifications that make a difference.

Sharing the Message

John Paul II teaches that one of the primary purposes of the body is "to make visible the invisible mystery of God." I realized after my deeper immersion in the Theology of the Body that, as a teacher of the faith, I, too, was called to make visible the invisible mysteries of God to the audiences to whom I was speaking. Commentators are a bit like artists, reading the canvas of the audience and communicating in such a way that brings about the result we intend. I believe that the

---

[7] Sheen, p. 35.

Theology of the Body is the delivery system par excellence of the sum total of the Christian mystery.

The devil wants to bring about disintegration in all areas of faith and life. The Theology of the Body is about integration. In fact, it is the Catholic sacramental worldview, in which the physical and spiritual are wedded. I live the Theology of the Body more fruitfully by performing the corporal works of mercy and other acts of charity. Even in the simple act of preaching and teaching, I am living out the spousal or "donative" meaning of my body by seeking to give myself to others.

Although the serious moral decline of our culture in undeniable, God has given us the great gift of John Paul II's Theology of the Body to minister to those who are hurting and to respond to those steeped in error. The tide is turning; we are beginning to reclaim God's original plan for humanity, particularly in the area of sexuality. The Theology of the Body has engaged us in a sabotage mission because its language is not the typical "legalism" that the world would expect from Christianity. It is remarkably refreshing language that acknowledges the partial truths that those in error have identified. John Paul II gave us the "theological time bomb," according to the words of George Weigel. The permissive culture has many casualties, but its darkness has not overcome the light. We laity must pick up this mantle and go forward. Our victory is guaranteed. In the words of John Paul II, "Do not be afraid." Christ will be with us.

Jesse Romero holds a bachelor's degree in liberal arts from Mount St Mary's College in Los Angeles and a master's degree in theology from Franciscan University of Steubenville in Ohio. As the proud parents of Paul, AnnMarie, and Joshua, Jesse and his wife Anita have been happily married for twenty-five years.

What Is the Theology of the Body?

Christopher West

*It is an illusion to think we can build a true culture of human life if we
do not . . . accept and experience sexuality and love and the whole of life
according to their true meaning and their close inter-connection.*
— John Paul II, *The Gospel of Life*, 97

The sexual embrace is the foundation stone of human life. The
family — and, in turn, human society itself — spring from this
embrace. In short, as sex goes, so go marriage and the family. As
marriage and the family go, so goes civilization.

Such logic doesn't bode well for our culture. It is no exaggeration
to say that the task of the twentieth century was to rid itself of the
Christian sexual ethic. If we're to build a "culture of life," the task of
the twenty-first century must be to reclaim it.

But the often repressive approach of previous generations
of Christians (usually silence or, at most, "don't do it") is largely
responsible for the cultural jettison of the Church's teaching on
sex. We need a "new language" to break the silence and reverse the
negativity. We need a fresh theology that explains how the Christian
sexual ethic — far from the prudish list of prohibitions it is assumed
to be — corresponds perfectly with the deepest yearnings of our hearts
for love and union.

As many people are only now discovering, Pope John Paul II

devoted the first major teaching project of his pontificate to developing just such a theology; he calls it a "theology of the body." This collection of 129 short talks has already begun a "sexual counter-revolution" that's changing lives around the world. The "fire" is spreading and in due time we can expect global repercussions.

Papal biographer George Weigel said it best when he described the theology of the body as "a kind of theological time bomb set to go off with dramatic consequences ...perhaps in the twenty-first century" (*Witness to Hope*, 343).

A Reply to Our Universal Questions

By focusing on the beauty of God's plan for the union of the sexes, John Paul shifts the discussion from legalism ("How far can I go before I break the law?") to liberty ("What's the truth that sets me free to love?"). The truth that sets us free is salvation in Jesus Christ. It doesn't matter what mistakes we've made or what sins we've committed. The Pope's theology of the body wags a finger at no one. It is a message of sexual salvation offered to one and all.

In short, through an in-depth reflection on the Scriptures, John Paul seeks to answer two of the most important, universal questions: (1) "What's it mean to be human?" and (2) "How do I live my life in a way that brings true happiness and fulfillment?" The Pope's teaching, therefore, isn't just about sex and marriage. Since our creation as male and female is the "fundamental fact of human existence" (February 13, 1980), the theology of the body affords "the rediscovery of the meaning of the whole of existence, the meaning of life" (October 29, 1980).

To answer the first question – "What's it mean to be human?" – the Pope follows Christ's invitation to reflect on the three different "stages" of the human experience of sex and the body: in our origin before sin (see Matthew 19:3-8); in our history darkened by sin yet redeemed in Christ (see Matthew 5:27-28); and in our destiny when God will raise our bodies in glory (see Matthew 22:23-33).

In response to the second question – "How do I live my life?" – John Paul applies his distinctive "Christian humanism" to the vocations of celibacy and marriage. He then concludes by demonstrating how his study provides a new, winning explanation of Church teaching on sexual morality.

We will look briefly at each of these different sections of the Pope's teaching. Of course, in a short introduction such as this, we're only scratching the surface of the Pope's profound insights (see resource section to learn more). We'll begin with his main idea.

Why is the Body a "Theology"?

According to John Paul II, God created the body as a "sign" of his own divine mystery. This is why he speaks of the body as a "theology," a study of God.

We can't see God. As pure Spirit, He is invisible. Yet Christianity is the religion of God's self-disclosure. In Christ, "God has revealed his innermost secret: God himself is an eternal exchange of love, Father, Son, and Holy Spirit, and he has destined us to share in that exchange" (CCC, n. 221). Somehow the human body makes this eternal mystery of love visible.

How? Specifically through the beauty of sexual difference and our call to union. God designed the union of the sexes as a "created version" of his own "eternal exchange of love." And right from the beginning, the union of man and woman foreshadows our eternal destiny of union with Christ. As St. Paul says, the "one flesh" union is "a great mystery, and I mean in reference to Christ and the church" (Ephesians 5:31-32).

The Bible uses spousal love more than any other image to help us understand God's eternal plan for humanity. God's wants to "marry" us (see Hosea 2:19) – to live with us in an "eternal exchange of love." And he wanted this great "marital plan" to be so plain to us, so obvious to us that he impressed an image of it in our very being by creating us male and female and calling us to communion in "one flesh."

Thus, in a dramatic development of Catholic thought, John Paul concludes that we image God not only as individuals, "but also through the communion ... which man and woman form right from the beginning." And, the Pope adds, "On all of this, right from 'the beginning,' there descended the blessing of fertility" (November 14, 1979). The original vocation to be "fruitful and multiply" (Genesis 1:28), then, is nothing but a call live in the image in which we're made – to love as God loves.

Of course, this doesn't mean God is "sexual." We use spousal love only as an analogy to help us understand something of the divine mystery (see CCC, n. 370). God's "mystery remains transcendent in regard to this analogy as in regard to any other analogy" (September 29, 1982). At the same time, however, the Pope says that there "is no other human reality which corresponds more, humanly speaking, to that divine mystery" (December 30, 1988).

The Original Experience of the Body and Sex

We tend to think the "war" between the sexes is normal. In his discussion with the Pharisees, Jesus points out that "from the beginning it was not so" (Matthew 19:8). Before sin, man and woman experienced their union as a participation in God's eternal love. This is the model for us all, and although we've fallen from this, Christ gives us real power to reclaim it.

The biblical creation stories use symbolic language to help us understand deep truths about ourselves. For example, the Pope observes that their original unity flows from the human being's experience of solitude. At first the man was "alone" (see Genesis 2:18). Among the animals there was no "helper fit for him" (Genesis 2:20). It's on the basis of this "solitude" – an experience common to male and female – that we experience our longing for union.

The point is that human sexual union differs radically from the mating of animals. If they were the same, Adam would have found plenty of "helpers" among the animals. But in naming the animals he realized he was different; he alone was a person called to love with his body in God's image. Upon sight of the woman the man immediately declares: "This at last is bone of my bones and flesh of my flesh" (Genesis 2:23). That's to say, "Finally, a person I can love."

How did he know that she too was a person called to love? Her naked body revealed the mystery! For the pure of heart, nakedness reveals what John Paul calls "the nuptial meaning of the body." This is the body's "capacity of expressing love: that love precisely in which the person becomes a gift and – by means of this gift – fulfills the very meaning of his being and existence" (January 16, 1980).

Yes, the Pope says if we live according to the truth of our sexuality, we fulfill the very meaning of life. What is it? Jesus reveals it when he says, "This is my commandment, that you love one another as I have loved you" (John 15:12). How did Jesus love us? "This is my body which is given for you" (Luke 22:19). God created sexual desire as the power to love as he loves. And this is how the first couple experienced it. Hence, they "were both naked, and were not ashamed" (Genesis 2:25).

There's no shame in love; "perfect love casts out fear" (I John 4:18). Living in complete accord with the nuptial meaning of their bodies, they saw and knew each other "with all the peace of the interior gaze, which creates the fullness of the intimacy of persons" (January 2, 1980).

The Historical Experience of the Body and Sex

Original sin caused the "death" of divine love in the human heart. The entrance of shame indicates the dawn of lust, of erotic desire void of God's love. Men and women of history now tend to seek "the sensation of sexuality" apart from the true gift of themselves, apart from authentic love.

We cover our bodies not because they're bad, but to protect their inherent goodness from the degradation of lust. Since we know we're made for love, we feel instinctively "threatened" not only by overt lustful behavior, but even by a "lustful look."

Christ's words are severe in this regard. He insists that if we look lustfully at others, we've already committed adultery in our hearts (see Matthew 5:28). John Paul poses the question: "Are we to fear the severity of these words, or rather have confidence in their salvific ... power?" (October 8, 1980). These words have power to save us because the man who utters them is "the Lamb of God, who takes away the sin of the world" (John 1:29).

Christ didn't die and rise from the dead merely to give us coping mechanisms for sin. "Jesus came to restore creation to the purity of its origins" (CCC, n. 2336). As we open ourselves to the work of redemption, Christ's death and resurrection effectively "liberate our liberty from the domination of lust" as John Paul expresses it (March I, 1984).

On this side of heaven, we will always be able to recognize a battle in our hearts between love and lust. Even so, John Paul insists that "the redemption of the body" (see Romans 8:23) is already at work in men and women of history. This means as we allow our lusts to be "crucified with Christ" (see Galatians 5:24) we can progressively rediscover in what is erotic that original "nuptial meaning of the body" and live it. This "liberation from lust" and the freedom it affords is, in fact, "the condition of all life together in truth" (October 8, 1980).

The Ultimate Experience of the Body & Sex

What about our experience of the body in the resurrection? Didn't Christ say we'll no longer be given in marriage when we rise from the dead (see Matthew 22:30)? Yes, but this doesn't mean our longing for union will be done away with. It means it will be fulfilled. As a sacrament, marriage is only on earthly sign of the heavenly reality. We no longer need signs to point us to heaven, when we're in heaven. The "marriage of the Lamb" (Revelation 19:7)—the union of love we all desire—will be eternally consummated.

"For man, this consummation will be the final realization of the unity of the human race, which God willed from creation. ...Those who are united with Christ will form the community of the redeemed, 'the holy city' of God, 'the Bride, the wife of the Lamb'" (CCC, n. 1045). This eternal reality is what the "one flesh" union foreshadows from the beginning (see Ephesians 5:31-32).

Hence, in the resurrection of the body we rediscover—in an eternal dimension—the same nuptial meaning of the body in the meeting with the mystery of the living God face to face (see December 9, 1981). "This will be a completely new experience," the Pope says —beyond anything we can imagine. Yet "it will not be alienated in any way from what man took part in from 'the beginning,' nor from [what concerns] the procreative meaning of the body and of sex" (January 13, 1982).

The Christian Vocations

By looking at "who we are" in our origin, history, and destiny, we open the door to a proper understanding of the Christian vocations of celibacy and marriage. Both vocations are an authentic "living out" of the most profound truth of who we are as male and female.

When lived authentically, Christian celibacy isn't a rejection of sexuality and our call to union. It actually points to their ultimate fulfillment. Those who sacrifice marriage "for the sake of the kingdom" (Matthew 19:12) do so in order to devote all of their energies and desires to the marriage that alone can satisfy: the marriage of Christ and the Church. In a way, they're "skipping" the sacrament (the earthly sign) in anticipation of the ultimate reality. By doing so, celibate men and women declare to the world that the kingdom of God is here (see Matthew 12:28).

In a different way, marriage also anticipates heaven. "In the joys of their love [God gives spouses] here on earth a foretaste of the wedding feast of the Lamb" (CCC, n. 1642). Why, then, do so many couples experience marriage as a "living hell"? In order for marriage to bring the happiness it's meant to, spouses must live it as God intended "from the beginning." This means they must contend diligently with the effects of sin.

Marriage doesn't justify lust. As a sacrament, marriage is meant to symbolize the union of Christ and the Church (see Ephesians 5:31-32). The body has a "language" that's meant to express God's free, total, faithful, and fruitful love. This is exactly what spouses commit to at the altar. "Have you come here freely?" the priest asks, "to give yourselves to each other without reservation? Do you promise to be faithful until death? Do you promise to receive children lovingly form God?" Bride and groom say "yes."

In turn, spouses are meant to express this same "yes" with their bodies whenever they become one flesh. "Indeed the very words 'I take you to be my wife, my husband,'" the Pope says, "can be fulfilled only by means of conjugal intercourse" (January 5, 1983). Sexual union is meant to be the renewal of wedding vows!

A New Context for Understanding Sexual Morality

The Church's sexual ethic begins to make sense when viewed through this lens. It's not a prudish list of prohibitions. It's a call to embrace our own "greatness," our own God-like dignity. It's a call to live the love we're created for.

Since a prophet is one who proclaims God's love, John Paul II describes the body and sexual union as "prophetic." But, he adds, we must be careful to distinguish between true and false prophets. If we can speak the truth with our bodies, we can also speak lies. Ultimately all questions of sexual morality come down to one simple question: Does this truly image God's free, total, faithful, fruitful love or does it not?

In practical terms, how healthy would a marriage be if spouses were regularly unfaithful to their wedding vows? On the other hand, how healthy would a marriage be if spouses regularly renewed their vows, expressing an ever-increasing commitment to them? This is what's at stake in the Church's teaching on sexual morality.

Masturbation, fornication, adultery, intentionally sterilized sex, homosexual acts, etc. – none of these image God's free, total, faithful, and fruitful love. None of these behaviors express and renew wedding vows. They aren't marital. Does this mean people who behave in such ways are "inherently evil?" No. They're just confused about how to satisfy their genuine desires for love.

If I offered you a million dollar bill and a counterfeit million dollar bill, which would you prefer? Dumb question, I know. But what if you were raised in a culture that incessantly bombarded you with propaganda convincing you that counterfeit was the real thing and the real thing was a counterfeit? Might you be a little confused?

Authentic Sexual Liberation

Why all the propaganda? If there's an enemy that wants to keep us from heaven, and if the body and sex is meant to point us there, what do you think he's going to attack? Sin's tactic is to "twist" and "disorient" our desire for the eternal embrace. That's all it can do. When we understand this, we realize that the sexual confusion so prevalent in our world and in our own hearts is nothing but the human desire for heaven gone berserk.

But the tide is changing. People can only put up with the counterfeits for so long. Not only do they fail to satisfy, they wound us terribly. Sadly, the truth of the Church's teaching on sex is confirmed in the wounds of those who haven't lived it. Our longings for love, intimacy, and freedom are good. But the sexual revolution sold us a bill of goods. We haven't been "liberated." We've been duped, betrayed, and left wanting.

This is why the world is a mission field ready to soak up John Paul II's theology of the body. And this is why it's already changing so many lives around the world. The Pope's teaching helps us distinguish between the real million dollar bill and the counterfeit. It helps us "untwist" our disordered desires and orients us towards the love that truly satisfies.

As this happens, we experience the Church's teaching not as a burden imposed from "without," but as a message of salvation welling up from "within." We experience the truth that sets us free. In other words, we experience what the sexual revolution promised but couldn't deliver – authentic sexual liberation.

Theology of the Body Resources

The following is a partial list of resources and organizations that can assist you in your further study of John Paul II's Theology of the Body.

Resources by Christopher West

Books

> *Good News About Sex & Marriage: Answers to Your Honest Questions about Catholic Teaching* (Servant, 2000; revised ed., 2006)
>
> *Theology of the Body for Beginners: A Basic Introduction to Pope John Paul II's Sexual Revolution* (Ascension, 2003; revised ed., 2009)
>
> *Theology of the Body Explained: A Commentary on John Paul II's Man and Woman He Created Them* (Pauline, 2003; revised ed., 2007)
>
> *The Love That Satisfies: Reflections on Eros and Agape* (Ascension, 2007)
>
> *Heaven's Song: Sexual Love as It Was Meant to Be* (Ascension, 2008)

Audio & Video Presentations

An extensive collection of audio and video presentations by Christopher West are available for personal or group study from Ascension Press. Visit www.ChristopherWest.com or www.AscensionPress.com for more information or call 1-800-376-0520.

Official Website

> Visit ChristopherWest.com or TheologyoftheBody.com for information on Christopher's speaking schedule, downloadable articles and audio files, or to purchase any of his books and other resources.

Books, Tapes, and Other Resources

The GIFT Foundation

> This not-for-profit lay apostolate offers a variety of audio and video resources on the theology of the body, natural family planning, and related topics. Visit www.GiftFoundation.org or call (847) 844-1167.

Our Father's Will Communications

> Offers audio and video products by speakers like Katrina Zeno, David Sloan, Christopher West, and many more. Visit www. TheologyoftheBody.net or call 1-866-333-OFWC.

Pauline Books and Media

> The publishing apostolate of the Daughters of St. Paul, they publish John Paul II's *Theology of the Body: Human Love in the Divine Plan* and Christopher West's *Theology of the Body Explained: A Commentary on John Paul II's Man and Woman He Created Them.* Visit Pauline.org or call 1-800-876-4463.

Real Love Productions

> Books, videos, and other resources by Mary Beth Bonacci. In her dynamic presentations, Mary Beth draws from the Theology of the Body to support teens, young adults, and parents in their quest for a true understanding of what it means to love and be loved. Visit www.RealLove.net or call 1-888-667-4992.

Organizations

Family Honor

> Provides resources and programs based on the Theology of the Body to help parents and children grow together in their understanding of God's plan for life and human sexuality. Visit www.FamilyHonor.org or call 1-877-208-1353

Theology of the Body Evangelization Team (TOBET)

> Engages in activities of evangelization, apologetics, education, charity and mission through the use of various media with a focus on Pope John Paul II's theology of the body. Visit www.Tobet.org

Theology of the Body International Alliance (TOBIA)

> A support network providing resources for those striving to evangelize the world by means of Pope John Paul II's understanding of the human person, explained in his works Love and Responsibility and Theology of the Body. A great resource for help in starting a Theology of the Body study group. Visit TheologyoftheBody.net and click on the TOBIA link.

Theology of the Body Institute

> A non-profit apostolate promoting the Theology of the Body at the popular level of both the Christian and the secular cultures. Through graduate and undergraduate courses, seminars, workshops, books, articles, newsletters, pamphlets, audio and video recordings, and exposure in popular media such as newspapers, magazines, television, radio and the Internet, Theology of the Body Institute seeks to penetrate and permeate the culture with a vision of sexuality that appeals to the deepest yearnings of the human heart for love and union. Visit www.TOBInstitute.org or call 1-215-302-8200.

Women Affirming Life

> Offers *A New Language* study series on the Theology of the Body by Dr. Mary Shivanandan of the John Paul II Institute. This is a four-season group study series, each consisting of six weekly sessions. Visit www.AffirmLife.com or call (617) 254-2277.

Women of the Third Millennium (WTTM)

> A lay organization co-founded by Katrina Zeno and Zoe Romanowsky in response to John Paul II's call for women to develop a "new feminism." WTTM offers a variety of retreats for women and men. Visit www.wttm.org or call 1-740-282-9062.

Further Education/Training

Heart Mind and Strength University for Living (HMSU)

> HMSU offers online courses that are "part retreat, part seminar, part small faith group." Class size is strictly limited to ensure personal attention from your Instructor/Mentor as well as to afford plenty of opportunity to interact with other learners. Courses in the theology of the body and related subjects are available. Visit www.HMSU.com.

John Paul II Institute for Studies on Marriage & Family

> This pontifical institute is a graduate school of theology founded by Pope John Paul II to help the Church understand more fully the human person, marriage, and the family in light of divine revelation. Visit www.JohnPaulii.edu for the Washington, DC campus and www.JP2institute.org for the Australian campus.

Acknowledgments

- To each of the contributors to this book. Thank you for sharing your heart, your joys, and your struggles for the purpose of leading others to the freedom you now enjoy.

- To Lisa Likona, for your editorial assistance with this book, your excellent insights, and your "feminine genius," which came through in your counsel on many of the stories.

- To Ascension's managing editor, Mike Flickinger. What a comfort it is turning a manuscript in to you, knowing your prudence, skill, and love for the truth always results in a much better end product.

- To all the staff members of Ascension Press for your commitment and professionalism.

- To Lynn Klika and the staff of Catholic Word for your many years of extraordinary service and commitment.

About the Editor

M atthew Pinto is the author or co-author of several books, including the bestselling question-and-answer books *Did Adam and Eve Have Belly Buttons?* (Ascension, 1998), *Did Jesus Have a Last Name?* (Ascension, 2005), and *Do I Have to Go? 101 Questions about the Mass, the Eucharist, and Your Spiritual Life* (Ascension, 2007). The co-creator of the *Friendly Defenders* Catholic Flash Cards and the *Amazing Grace* series of books. Matt also co-wrote *A Guide to the Passion: 100 Questions about The Passion of the Christ,* which sold more than a million copies and reached number six on the *New York Times* Best-Seller List.

Matthew has appeared on numerous television and radio programs explaining and defending the Catholic faith, and he has conducted seminars on a variety of Catholic issues throughout the country. Matt and his wife, Maryanne, live in Chester County, Pennsylvania, and are the parents of five boys.